小學生 Grammar

圖解教程和練習

詞語文法

配合香港教育局建議學習目標編寫

小學二至五年級適用

編著 李雪熒

- 23篇圖解趣味詞語教程
- 覆蓋小學重點文法學習目標
- 69組不同程度練習（附答案）
- 讓各級學生輕鬆學好Grammar

序言

各位小朋友：

在香港讀書，你們無可避免要學好英文。無論你喜歡學英文，還是一見到雞腸般的英文句子就想找個洞去躲避，英文仍然無時無刻存在於你的學習和生活環境之中。總之，你是躲也躲不了的。既然是這樣，最好的方法，就是直接面對它。

你們或許會發現，有些同學英文學得很輕鬆，有些卻學得很辛苦，某同學的英文考試成績總是非常優異，而自己和另一些同學卻普普通通。為甚麼會這樣呢？是不是那些學得較好的同學較聰明呢？當然不是！其實，只要大家學英文時，懂得靈活運用，融會貫通，平時多留意身邊事物，如零食包裝上的英文、地鐵車廂裡或廣告上標示的英文，再結合老師在課堂上教的文法知識，你就會覺得學英文是一件輕鬆愉快的事情。

為了幫助大家學好英文，本書在教授各種文法時，不但為你詳細剖析句子的文法結構，而且還提供大量例句，鞏固你的文法知識。大家掌握了文法知識後，不妨到「文法加油站」做一些練習；你還可以到「挑戰站」挑戰難度較高的題目，一試身手。

有了這本書，學英文Grammar，從此變得很輕鬆！

李雪熒

作者簡介

李雪熒，香港中文大學社會科學榮譽學士及北京師範大學文學碩士，深信學習是一場愉快的遊戲，曾任創意寫作班、繪畫班、校本學習支援導師，著有《學生專題研習天書》、《我的第一本經典英文100童詩》、《小學生學理財經濟55通識課》、《彈升孩子學習戰鬥力》、《睡前德育小故事——100教訓》、《中國謀略故事》、《親子枕邊100成語故事III》、《高效孩子的12個習慣》、《戒掉孩子壞習慣》、《態度決定孩子一生》、《生活細節教出大道理》等。

目　錄
Table of Contents

chapter 1

認識名詞：可數與不可數

Nouns: Countable and Uncountable

盈盈和安琪在玩「名詞」遊戲，到底誰會勝出呢？安琪在白板上寫下「apple」（蘋果），盈盈則寫出「apples」；接着，盈盈寫出「milk」（牛奶），安琪寫出「milks」。盈盈立即高聲呼叫：「你輸了！」安琪為甚麼輸了呢？到底他們在玩甚麼遊戲？

其實，名詞（Nouns）是人、動物、地方及各種事物的名稱，例如：「man」（男人）、「dog」（狗）、「gun」（槍）、「hat」（帽子）、「shirt」（襯衫）、「Hong Kong」（香港）、「Tony」（東尼）等等。名詞又可分為可數名詞（Countable nouns）與不可數名詞（Uncountable nouns）。

可數名詞

可數的名詞是指能數算的事物，可以是單數（Singular），即一個，也可以是複數（Plural），即兩個或以上，例如：「apple」是可數的單數名詞，而「apples」則是可數的複數名詞。下表有更多的例子：

單數（Singular）	複數（Plural）
egg（雞蛋）	eggs
girl（女孩）	girls
pen（筆）	pens
box（箱子）	boxes
fish（魚）	fishes
baby（嬰兒）	babies
puppy（小狗）	puppies
fly（蒼蠅）	flies
knife（刀）	knives
leaf（葉子）	leaves
thief（小偷）	thieves

名詞的尾巴

大家留心觀察這個單數和複數名詞表，有沒有發現複數名詞一欄的名詞，有些尾部加「s」，有些則加「es」、「ies」和「ves」呢？大部分名詞，如要表示複數，通常在詞尾加「s」即可，但有些名詞，由於發音的關係，表示複數時，就要加「es」、「ies」和「ves」。

以「s」、「ss」、「ch」、「sh」、「x」結尾的名詞，表示複數時，就要在字詞的尾部加「es」，例如「glasses」（眼鏡）、「watches」（手錶）等等。

以「輔音＋o」結尾的名詞，表示複數時，就要在字詞的尾部加「es」，如「tomatoes」（番茄）、「potatoes」（馬鈴薯）、「heroes」（英雄）；而「元音＋o」結尾的名詞，表示複數時，只需在字詞的尾部直接加「s」，如「radios」（收音機）、「zoos」（動物園）、「pianos」（鋼琴），但「photos」（照片）是例外的。

以「輔音字母＋y」結尾的名詞，表示複數時，就要在字詞的尾部先將「y」改為「i」再加「es」，例如「cherries」（櫻桃）、「cities」（城市）等等。大家要留意，有些名詞，如「boy」（男孩），由於「y」在字詞中的發音跟「cherry」不同，因此，表示複數時，「boy」不能寫成「boies」，而應該寫作「boys」。

以「f」或「fe」結尾的名詞，表示複數時，就要將「f」或「fe」改為「v」再加「es」，例如「wolves」（狼）、「shelves」（擱架）等等。

除此之外，也有一些複數名詞的特殊例子，大家要好好記住啊！例如右表：

特殊例子

單數（Singular）	複數（Plural）
child（孩子）	children
man（男人）	men
woman（女人）	women
policeman（警員）	policemen
goose（鵝）	geese
mouse（老鼠）	mice
foot（腳）	feet
tooth（牙齒）	teeth

複數名詞尾部變化簡表

名詞	複數的尾部變化	例子
一般名詞	加「s」	cat（貓）▶ cats
「元音＋o」結尾的名詞	加「s」	radio（收音機）▶radios
以「輔音＋o」結尾的名詞	加「es」	mango（芒果）▶ mangoes
以「s」、「ss」、「ch」、「sh」、「x」結尾的名詞	加「es」	bus（巴士）▶ buses
以「輔音字母＋y」結尾的名詞	加「ies」	library（圖書館）▶libraries
以「f」或「fe」結尾的名詞	加「ves」	scarf（圍巾）▶ scarves wife（妻子）▶ wives

不可數名詞

至於不可數名詞是指不能數算的事物，是沒有單數和複數的。例如：

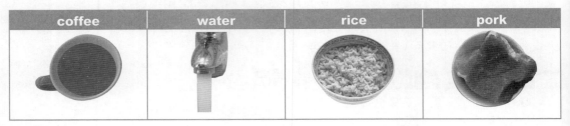

coffee	water	rice	pork
			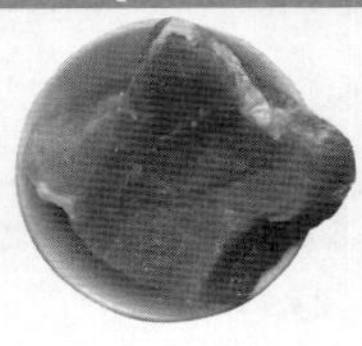

集合名詞

另外，名詞之中，有一些是集合名詞（Collective nouns）。一些同類的事物、人物等，可以集合成一個單位，成為集合名詞。集合名詞可以表示單數，也可以表示複數。例如：「family」（家庭）由數個家庭成員組成，因此是集合名詞；再例如「audience」（觀眾），很多人在同一個場合或時間觀賞同一個表演或節目，因此是集合名詞。其他集合名詞有：「army」（軍隊）、「crowd」（人群）、「team」（隊伍）等等。

Family

單數、可數的名詞不能單獨使用，通常要加上冠詞（Articles），即「a」、「an」、「the」。例如「the sun」、「an apple」、「a pig」等等。不可數的名詞不能加上「a」和「an」，例如「water」☑，「a water」☒。

注意專有名詞（Proper nouns），包括地名和人名，是沒有複數的，例如「Italy」（義大利），大家不要一看到最後的字母是「y」，於是寫成「Italies」，這是錯的。另外，名詞中的地名、人名，它的第一個字母必須是大寫（Capital letter），例如：「China」（中國）、「America」（美國）、「Chinese」（中國人）、「Causeway Bay」（銅鑼灣）、「Tsim Sha Tsui」（尖沙嘴）、「Stella」（斯特拉）、「Tom」（湯姆）等等。

文法加油站

練習一

以下名詞哪些是可數的？哪些是不可數的？請在可數名詞的方格上寫上「C」，不可數名詞的方格上寫上「U」。

1.water		6.book		11.bird	
2.woman		7.library		12.money	
3.teacher		8.school		13.rice	
4.sugar		9.bread		14.ink	
5.pig		10.butter		15.box	

練習二

請將下列單數名詞改為複數。

單數 (Singular)	複數 (Plural)	單數 (Singular)	複數 (Plural)
例子: apple	apples	8. bag	
1. rabbit		9. party	
2. orange		10. thief	
3. wife		11. flower	
4. watch		12. wish	
5. hero		13. dish	
6. book		14. baby	
7. pencil		15. year	

挑戰站

請參看例子，找出下列名詞中的錯誤，並將正確的答案寫在右邊的方格內。

例子：

cates <u>cats</u>

knifes <u>knives</u>

1. sisteres		9. traines	
2. cupes		10. doctores	
3. uncleies		11. Italies	
4. beeives		12. Hong Kongs	
5. balles		13. Peters	
6. tomatos		14. dressies	
7. universitys		15. Chinas	
8. busives			

chapter 2

人物代名詞：

我、你、她

Pronouns: Personal pronouns

媽媽帶方方上街，在文具店裡，方方指着一個咪咪貓筆盒，說：「It is very beautiful. I like it.」（它很好看，我喜歡它。）在寵物店看到一隻可愛的小狗時，說「It is lovely.」（牠很可愛。）過了一會兒，方方突然大叫：「Oh, he is so cute. I want him.」（噢！他很可愛，我要他。）媽媽覺得奇怪，方方到底在說甚麼？「他」是誰？

大家有沒有留意方方所說的每句話都含有代名詞（Pronouns）。代名詞是指替代名詞（Nouns）的字詞，例如：「John」可以用「He」（他）來代替；「Amanda」可以用「She」（她）來代替、「The dog」、「The pen」可以用「It」（牠/它）來代替、「Sam and Stella」可以用「They」（他們）來代替，等等，而方方所用的代名詞稱為人物代名詞（Personal pronouns）。

甚麼是人物代名詞？

人物代名詞（Personal pronouns）是用來替代名詞的，包括「I」（我）、「He」（他）、「She」（她）、「It」（牠）、「They」（他們）、「We」（我們）、「You」（你/你們）、「me」（我）、「him」（他）、「her」（她）、「us」（我們）、「you」（你/你們）、「them」（他們），例如：

Joey and Sam are classmates.
They study together.
祖兒和森姆是同學。他們一起學習。

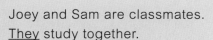

句式放大鏡

Joey and Sam | are | classmates. | They | study | together.

主詞（名詞） | 動詞 | 代名詞

在「Joey and Sam are classmates. They study together.」這兩個句子裡，第二句的人物代名詞「They」是用來代替第一句的主詞「Joey and Sam」的。一般來說，如果前面的句子已帶出主詞，後面的句子在講述同一人物或事物時，可以使用人物代名詞（Personal pronouns）來代替。例如：

Mandy is my sister. She likes playing tennis.
曼迪是我的姐姐。她喜歡打網球。

Benjamin and I are good friends. We play football every Sunday.
本傑明和我是好朋友。我們每個星期天都踢足球。

此外，句中的受詞（Object）在適當的情形下也可以使用人物代名詞「me」、「him」、「her」、「it」、「you」、「us」、「them」來代替。例如：

Jack saw a kitten. He fed it some milk.
積克看到一隻小貓。他餵牠牛奶。

Miss Lee chose Amy and me for the competition.
李老師選了艾美和我參加比賽。

Miss Lee chose us for the competition.
李老師選了我們參加比賽。

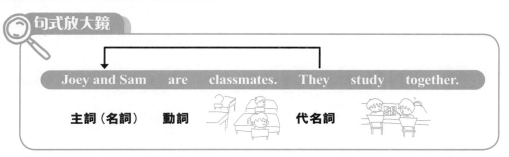

2 Pronouns: Personal pronouns

第一身、第二身、第三身和單數、複數

人物代名詞可分為第一身、第二身和第三身，其中又可各自分為單數和複數，大家不妨參看以下人物代名詞簡表：

			主詞 (Subject)	受詞 (Object)
第一身	單數		I (我)	me (我)
	複數		We (我們)	us (我們)
第二身	單數		You (你)	you (你)
	複數		You (你們)	you (你們)
第三身	單數		He (他)	him (他)
	單數		She (她)	her (她)
	單數		It (牠/它)	it (牠/它)
	複數		They (他們)	them (他們)

使用人物代名詞時，要留意主詞的性別；是單數，還是複數；以及是生物，還是死物。

文法加油站

練習一

參看例子，圈出正確的答案。

例子：My sister is watching TV. (They/ She) is not doing homework.

1. Look at the dog. (He / It) has a long tail.
2. This is my father. (She / He) is a fireman.
3. Kitty and Amy are my friends. (She / They) like playing piano.
4. (We / You) are a boy. Your name is Frankie.
5. Amy's daddy brought (it / her) a picture book.
6. I need some water. Please give (I / me) some.
7. The children help themselves. (We / They) are smart children.
8. Peggy and I are good friends. (We / They) go to swim every Saturday.
9. Sandy and Ray are in the music room. (You / They) are singing.
10. The cat is sleeping. (We / It) likes fish.

練習二

參看例子，找出句中的人物代名詞所代表的事物。

例子：My sister is reading a book. It is very interesting.

My sister is reading a book. It is very interesting.

1. Look at the dog. John is feeding it .
2. May has an apple. She will eat it after lunch.
3. Ken and Jerry are my friends. They like playing football.
4. The boy is making a car model. It will be finished later.
5. Annie is good at singing. Miss Wong chose her for the singing competition.
6. I need some pepper. Please pass it to me.
7. Johnny helps himself. He is a smart boy.
8. Peggy and Penny are good at painting. They will paint at the park this Sunday.
9. The pandas are cute. Let's take some photos for them.
10. The chess class is fun. It was taught by Mr. Lam.

挑戰站

找出下列句子中的錯誤，將正確的答案寫在右面的橫線上。

例子：

Daddy will go to America tomorrow. (She) will stay there for a week. He

1. This is my birthday present. They is presented by daddy. ______
2. Tom and Sandy swam in the swimming pool yesterday. We were very happy. ______
3. Kelly loves her grandpa so much. He will visit him tomorrow. ______
4. We are going to have a barbecue this Sunday. Will you join them? ______
5. Some people are in the park. He are doing exercises. ______
6. Tom and Sammy will see the movie tomorrow. She is about a romantic story. ______
7. Frankie is washing dishes. She are very dirty. ______
8. You is my brother. His name is Bobby. ______
9. The dog is chasing another dog. He runs fast. ______
10. Tommy is working in ABC company. He is a trading firm. ______

chapter 3

反身代名詞：為自己而做的

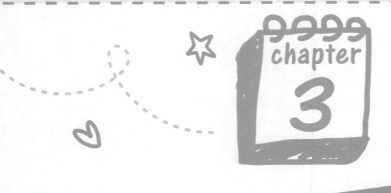

Pronouns: Reflexive pronouns

方方和小朋友上街去，他們在路上看到一隻小貓，方方說：「Look! The cat scratches itself.」（看，那隻小貓給自己搔癢。）在快餐店，店員姐姐跟方方和她的朋友說：「Welcome, please help yourselves.」（歡迎，請你們自己取餐。）

大家有沒有留意方方和店員姐姐所說的話都含有代名詞（Pronouns）中的反身代名詞（Reflexive pronouns）。英語的反身代名詞有：myself（我自己）、himself（他自己）、herself（她自己）、itself（牠自己）、yourself（你自己）、yourselves（你們自己）、ourselves（我們自己）、themselves（他們自己）。

甚麼是反身代名詞？

甚麼時候可以使用反身代名詞（Reflexive pronouns）呢？**當行動的人做的動作是為自己而做時，就可以使用反身代名詞，以強調是為指定的人而做的。**例如：

I cook for myself.
我為自己做飯。

Nancy dresses herself.
南茜為自己裝扮。

The boy helps himself.
那個男孩自己幫助自己。

The cat scratches itself.
那隻貓自己抓自己。

Please help yourselves.
請你們自己幫助自己。

We encourage ourselves.
我們鼓勵我們自己。

Sam and Judy made themselves some apple pies.
山姆和茱迪給他們自己做了一些蘋果餡餅。

「Nancy dresses herself.」一句使用了「herself」來強調「dresses」（裝扮）這個動作是做動作者Nancy對自己做的。大家使用反身代名詞時，記得留意主詞與反身代名詞要一致，例如主詞是「He」，就要使用「himself」，而不能使用「herself」或其他反身代名詞。

第一身、第二身和第三身

另外，反身代名詞可分為第一身、第二身和第三身。大家看看以下簡表：

		主詞	反身代名詞
第一身	單數	I	myself （我自己）
	複數	We	ourselves（我們自己）
第二身	單數	You	yourself（你自己）
	複數	You	yourselves（你們自己）
第三身	單數	He	himself（他自己）
		She	herself（她自己）
		It	itself（牠自己）
	複數	They	themselves（他/她/牠們自己）

文法加油站

練習一

參看例子，圈出正確的答案。

例子：We help (themselves/ ourselves) in supermarket.

1. Look! The monkey is scratching (himself / itself).
2. The panda is playing (herself / itself) with the ball.
3. Kitty made (itself / herself) some sandwiches.
4. You should help (yourself / themselves) for the homework.
5. This is buffet. Please help (themselves / yourself).
6. We made (ourselves / myself) some drinks.
7. The children help (ourselves / themselves) for the project.
8. I took (myself / itself) some photos with this digital camera.
9. Sandy drew (yourselves / herself) a picture.
10. The cat scratches (yourselves / itself).

練習二

參看例子，圈出句中的反身代名詞，並加箭咀指出其所指向的人物。

例子：Phoebe is making herself a cake.

Phoebe is making (herself) a cake.

1. Look at the dog. It is scratching itself.
2. Vicky is drawing herself a picture.
3. Jerry and Chris are helping themselves on the problem.
4. Tom is making himself a craft.
5. Annie is keeping herself calm for a few minutes.
6. I am making myself an apple pie.
7. Johnny is a smart boy. He solves the problem himself.
8. Penny is dressing herself.
9. The panda fed its child itself.
10. Teddy encourages himself for the competition.

挑戰站

找出下列句子中的錯處，將正確的答案寫在右邊。

例子：

Jerry is working hard for (herself). ____himself____

1. The cat is scratching itselves. ________
2. Bobby is making themselves some sandwiches. ________
3. Tammy is singing for yourself. ________
4. We entertain themselves. ________
5. The old man is looking for herself. ________
6. Jessica painted himself a picture. ________
7. Frankie is writing yourselves a letter. ________
8. You are taking ourselves a photo. ________
9. She is dressing himself for the party. ________
10. The children solved the problem himself. ________

chapter 4

指示代名詞：指出人和事物

Pronouns: Demonstrative pronouns

方方看到遠處有一隻狗，說：「That is a big dog.」（那是一隻大狗。）美兒看到遠處有一些樹，說：「Those are mango trees」（那些是芒果樹。）

方方和美兒在公園裡看到很多事物呢！大家有沒有留意她們所說的話都含有代名詞（Pronouns）中的指示代名詞（Demonstrative pronouns）。

指示代名詞怎樣應用？

英語中的指示代名詞（Demonstrative pronouns）包括「this」（這個）、「that」（那個）、「these」（這些）、「those」（那些），主要用來指出人和事物。當所指示的人和事物距離說話人較近時，就要使用「This」或「These」；當所指示的人和事物距離說話人較遠時，就要使用「That」或「Those」。例如：

This is a book.
這是一本書。

That is a cat.
那是一隻貓。

These are flowers.
這些是花。

Those are trees.
那些是樹。

單數和複數

除了留意所指示的人和事物跟說話人的距離外，也要留意所指示的人或事物的數量。指示代名詞有單數和複數之分，如果事物是單數（即一個），就要使用「this」或「that」，如果事物是複數（即兩個或以上），就要使用「these」或「those」。例如：

This is a policeman.
這是一位警察。

These are policemen.
這些是警察。

That is a pig.
那是一隻豬。

Those are pigs.
那些是豬。

使用指示代名詞要留意所指事物的數量（是單數，還是複數？），以及所指的事物跟説話人的距離（是遠，還是近？）。

文法加油站

練習一

請在橫線上填上正確的指示代名詞。

1. __________ is a present for my grandpa.
2. ______________ are my brothers.
3. ______________ is an interesting movie.
4. ______________ are flowers.
5. ______________ was a wonderful trip.
6. ______________ are postmen.
7. ______________ is a big garden.
8. ________________ are expensive watches.
9. ________________ are my friends.
10. __________________ is Alison, my good friend.

練習二

請圈出正確的答案。

1. (These / This) are my books.
2. (That / Those) is my classmate.
3. (This / These) is a funny game.
4. (That / These) is a pig. Look! It is sleeping.
5. (That / Those) is my school.
6. (That / These) is my dog. Its name is Bobby.
7. (This / Those) are my toys.
8. (That / These) is his car. It is very expensive.
9. (Those / That) are my relatives. They visit us.
10. (This / Those) is Mr. Chan. He is my teacher.

挑戰站

請在橫線上填上正確的代名詞，包括人物代名詞、反身代名詞和指示代名詞。

1. My uncle is a doctor. ________ is not a lawyer.
2. I love my mommy. She loves ________ too.
3. Sally is not well. ________ has a cold.
4. He has hurt ________ by accident.
5. The TV is not working. ________ has broken down.
6. Judy and Lily lost the game. ________ are very sad.
7. Anna told me the news ________ .
8. Miss Lee is our teacher. She is so nice to ______ .
9. _______ is Alice. She is my sister.
10. ________ are my books. They are very interesting.

chapter 5

屬有名詞：誰是擁有者

Possession: Possessive nouns

維維和明明在課室裡，課室裡有不同的物品，這些物品是誰的？維維說：「This is Tommy's pencil box.」（這是湯美的筆盒。）明明說：「This is teacher's desk.」（這是老師的桌子。）維維說：「This is Danny's book.」（這是丹尼爾的書。）明明說：「This is Sam's bag.」（這是山姆的書包。）

維維和明明都知道哪些物品屬於哪個人，用來表示某物品屬於某人時，要使用屬有格（Possession）。維維和明明所說的話使用了屬有格中的屬有名詞（Possessive nouns），用來表示某人擁有某些物品。

單數屬有名詞

屬有名詞(Possessive nouns)是其中一種名詞，**用來表達某人/某些人擁有某(些)物品。**屬有名詞可分為單數屬有名詞和複數屬有名詞，單數屬有名詞的寫法是「單數名詞+'s」，如「Tammy's book」(譚美的書)、「the girl's bag」(那個女孩的書)、「the dog's house」(那隻狗的屋)，等等。

句式放大鏡

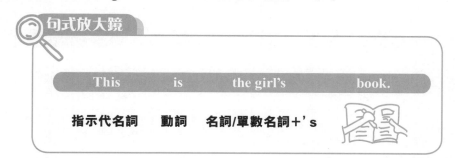

This	is	the girl's	book.
指示代名詞	動詞	名詞/單數名詞+'s	

在「This is the girl's book.」這個句子裡，「the girl」是單數名詞，在表達圖書是屬於那個女孩時，就要在名詞後接「's」，變成「the girl's book」。其他例子有：

This is a boy's room.
這是一個男孩的房間。

Sally's shoes are very beautiful.
莎莉的鞋子很漂亮。

These are Tammy's books.
這些是譚美的書。

複數屬有名詞

複數屬有名詞的寫法是「s結尾的名詞/複數名詞+'」，如「the girls' bags」(女孩們的手袋)、「some pandas' food」(一些熊貓的食物)，等等。

句式放大鏡

These	are	the girl's	toys .
指示代名詞	動詞	名詞/單數名詞+'s	

在「These are the girls' toys.」這個句子裡，「the girls」是複數名詞，在表達玩具是屬於女孩們時，就要在複數名詞後接「'」，變成「the girls' toys」。其他例子有：

These are the boys' toys.
這些是男孩們的玩具。

Those are the men's clothes.
那些是男士們的服裝。

屬於物件的部分

至於表達非生物所屬的部分，可以使用「....... of ....」來表示，如「the top of the tree」（樹的頂部）、「the wheels of the car」（一輛車的輪子）等等。

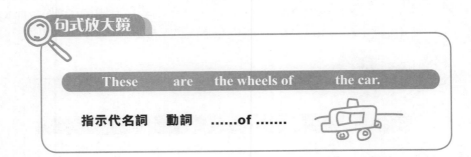

句式放大鏡

These	are	the wheels of	the car.
指示代名詞	動詞	......of	

在「These are the wheels of the car.」這個句子裡，由於汽車是非生物，在表達輪子是屬於汽車時，就要使用「.......of......」，變成「the wheels of the car」。

其他例子有：This is the title of the book.
這是書的名稱。

This is the door of the room.
這是房間的門。

These are the legs of the chair.
這些是椅子的腳。

文法加油站

練習一

參看例子，用屬有名詞改寫以下句子。

例子：These are the children models. These are the children’s models.

1. Mommy is cleaning Kitty room.
2. This is my father car.
3. Tracy borrowed Miss Lee book.
4. The boys English teacher is Mr. Smith.
5. Karen daddy brought her a computer game.
6. Kathy mommy goes to the supermarket.
7. This is Teddy dog.
8. I am using Kerry mobile.
9. Peter sister is Sue.
10. That is Amy watch.

練習二

參看例子，用屬有名詞改寫以下句子。

例子：A table has four legs. These are the legs of the table.

1. A bottle has two holes.

____

2. A chair has four legs.

____

3. A game has ten characters.

____

4. A magazine has a cover.

____

5. A flat has four windows.

____

6. A house has two doors.

____

7. A dog has two ears.

____

8. A car has four wheels.

____

9. A garden has many flowers.

____

10. A film has an end.

____

挑戰站

找出下列句子中的錯誤，將正確的答案寫在右面的橫線上。

例子：

Jerry car is blue. Jerry's car

This is the table's leg . the legs of the table

1. This is Cherry room. ______________

2. This is the roof on the house. ______________

3. The dog tail is long. ______________

4. This is the bed's legs. ______________

5. The old man grandchild is Mandy. ______________

6. Jessica picture is very beautiful. ______________

7. These are Fred toy cars. ______________

8. This is the book's cover. ______________

9. Those are the car's wheels. ______________

10. The children story books are there. ______________

chapter 6

屬有形容詞：我的、你的、他們的

Possession: Possessive Adjectives

恆恆和浩浩在客廳玩耍，過了一會兒，二人吵起來，而且不准對方玩自己的玩具。恆恆生氣地說：「This is my toy car.」（這是我的玩具車。）浩浩也不甘示弱，大聲地說：「This is my picture book.」（這是我的圖畫書。）結果，恆恆和浩浩整天都不理睬對方。

恆恆和浩浩吵架時所說的話都使用了屬有格（Possession）中的屬有形容詞（Possessive adjectives），用來表示某人擁有某些物品。

甚麼是屬有形容詞？

常見的屬有形容詞（Possessive Adjectives）包括：「my」（我的）、「his」（他的）、「her」（她的）、「its」（牠的）、「their」（他們的）、「our」（我們的）、「your」（你的/你們的），都是**用來表達某東西是屬於某人或某動物的形容詞，通常放在名詞前面**，即「屬有形容詞＋名詞」，如「my car」（我的車）、「your photo」（你的照片）、「their school」（他們的學校），例如：「This is my cup.」（這是我的杯子。）

句式放大鏡

This	is	my	cup.
指示代名詞	動詞	屬有形容詞	

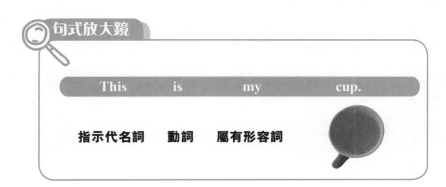

在「This is my cup.」這個句子裡，由於茶杯是名詞，在表達茶杯是屬於某人時，可以使用「屬有形容詞＋名詞」，即「my cup」（我的茶杯）或「your cup」（你的茶杯），等等。其他例子有：

My sister is a baby.
我的妹妹是嬰兒。

Our school is very clean.
我們的學校很乾淨。

Your mother is very beautiful.
你的媽媽很漂亮。

His name is Jackson.
他的名字是積臣。

Mr. Wong is her teacher.
黃先生是她的老師。

Bobby is my dog. This is its house.
波比是我的狗。這是牠的狗屋。

Their home is very big.
他們的家很大。

使用屬有形容詞時，要留意事物所屬者的性別，以及是單數，還是複數。而且，屬有形容詞只適用於生物，不能用於非生物。

文法加油站

練習一

參考例子，用屬有形容詞改寫句子。

例子：

I have a birthday present.

This is my birthday present.

1. My brother has a car model.

____

2. Sandy has a house.

____

3. A dog has a dog house.

____

4. Sam and Cathy have a car.

____

5. We have two computers.

____

6. You have two bags.

____

7. I have some books.

____

8. They have a boat.

____

9. The children have many toys.

____

10. May and you have many pictures.

____

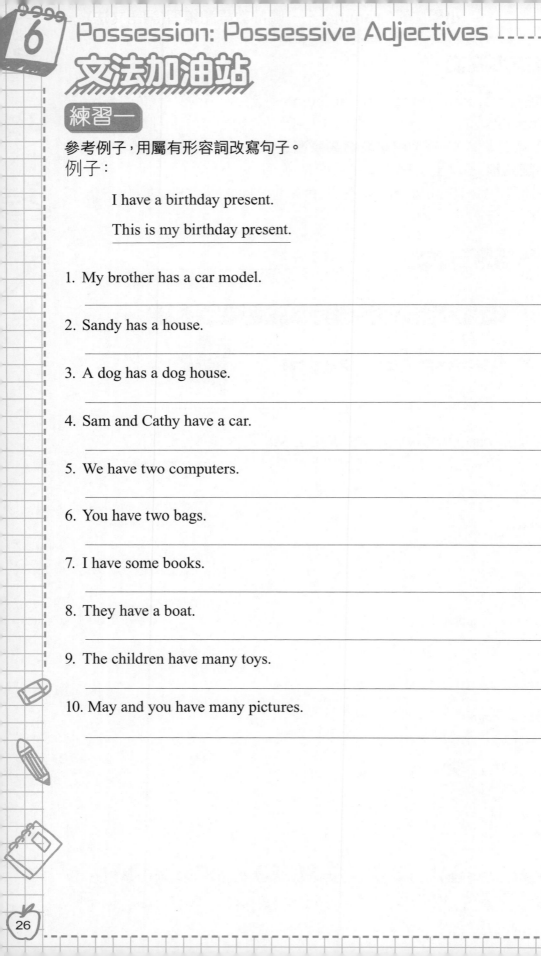

練習二

請圈出正確的答案。

1. Cherry and Kerry have a big house. This is (his / her / their) house.
2. Amy and Chris have a child. This is (your / their / its) child.
3. Miranda has a book. That is (his / our / her) book.
4. We have a computer. This is (their / our / your) computer.
5. Amy has a piano. That is (her / our / its) piano.
6. John has a cat. This is (his / her / its) cat.
7. Bobby is my dog. This is (his / her / its) house.
8. Grandpa has some books. These are (your / his / her) books.
9. I have a car model. That is (its / my / your) car model.
10. This is my grandma. (Her / His / My) name is Kathy.

挑戰站

找出下列句子中的錯誤，將正確的答案寫在右面的橫線上。

例子：

His name is Peter. I am a pupil. My

Ken has a desk. This is her desk. his

1. We have a big classroom. This is their classroom. ______
2. Grandma has a beautiful garden. This is his garden. ______
3. The dog has a long tail. His tail is brown. ______
4. I have a comfortable bed. This is your bed. ______
5. The old lady's bag is small. This is our bag. ______
6. June and Kelly have a beautiful picture. This is its picture. ______
7. Fanny has many toys. These are his toys. ______
8. I have a book. This is our book. ______
9. Shirley and Joe have a boat. This is his boat. ______
10. Miss Lee has a computer. This is their computer. ______

chapter 7

屬有代名詞：強調屬於誰的

Possession: Possessive pronouns

恆恆和浩浩又吵起來，不准對方碰自己的東西。恆恆生氣地說：「This is my pen. It is mine.」（這是我的筆。它是我的。）浩浩也不甘示弱，大聲地說：「This is my bag. It's mine.」（這是我的書包。它是我的。）恆恆激動地說：「This bag is mine. It is not yours. Your bag is there.」（這書包是我的。它不是你的。你的在那兒。）兩人都不服氣，結果打起架來。

恆恆和浩浩吵架時所說的話都使用了屬有格（Possession）中的屬有代名詞（Possessive pronouns），用來表示某些物品是屬於某人的。

屬有代名詞的用法

屬有代名詞（Possessive pronouns）包括：「mine」（我的）、「yours」（你的）、「his」（他的）、「hers」（她的）、「its」（牠的）、「theirs」（他們的）、「ours」（我們的），主要用來**表示某事物屬於某人**，在句中可用來取代由「屬有形容詞＋名詞」組成的字詞。例如：This is my bag. This is mine.

句式放大鏡

This	is	my	bag.	This	is	mine.
指示代名詞	動詞	屬有形容詞	名詞	指示代名詞	動詞	屬有代名詞

在「This is my bag. This is mine」這兩個句子裡，「my bag」是「屬有形容詞＋名詞」，因此可以以屬有代名詞「mine」來代替，表示句中所指的物件是屬於我的。其他例子有：

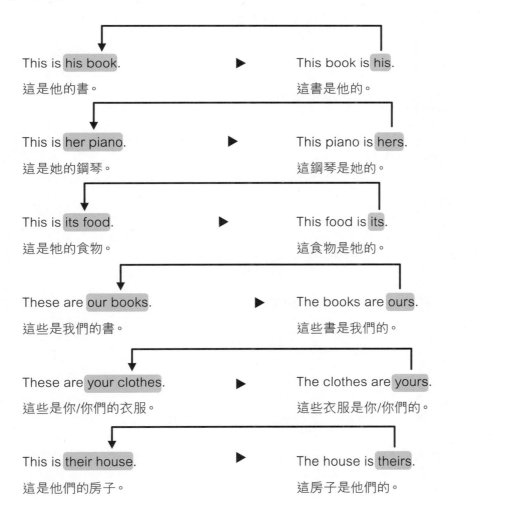

This is his book. ▶ This book is his.
這是他的書。 這書是他的。

This is her piano. ▶ This piano is hers.
這是她的鋼琴。 這鋼琴是她的。

This is its food. ▶ This food is its.
這是牠的食物。 這食物是牠的。

These are our books. ▶ The books are ours.
這些是我們的書。 這些書是我們的。

These are your clothes. ▶ The clothes are yours.
這些是你/你們的衣服。 這些衣服是你/你們的。

This is their house. ▶ The house is theirs.
這是他們的房子。 這房子是他們的。

文法加油站

練習一

參考例子，用屬有代名詞改寫句子。

例子：

I have a birthday present.

The birthday present is mine.

1. My brother has a car model.

____

2. Sandy has a house.

____

3. A dog has a dog house.

____

4. Sam and Cathy have a car.

____

5. We have two computers.

____

6. You have two bags.

____

7. I have some books.

____

8. They have a boat.

____

9. The children have many toys.

____

10. May and you have many pictures.

____

練習二

參看例子，圈出句中的屬有代名詞，並加箭咀指出其所指向的屬有者和事物。

例子：This is Tony's birthday cake. This is his.

This is <u>Tony's birthday cake</u>. This is (his).

1. This is my dog. This is mine.
2. This is Ricky's bag. This is his.
3. This is Jerry and Ann's house. This is theirs.
4. This is Tom's car model. This is his.
5. This is the dog's house. This is its.
6. This is my cup. This is mine.
7. These are your books. These are yours.
8. This is Penny's dress. This is hers.
9. That is Mr. Leung's car. That is his.
10. This is our house. This is ours.

挑戰站

請在橫線上填上正確的屬有名詞、屬有形容詞和屬有代名詞。

1. I have a boy friend. ___________ name is Raymond.
2. Mommy has some watches. The watches are ___________ .
3. Mr. Fong is Kelly ________ teacher.
4. I am Sally. Tom is _________ brother.
5. A TV has a screen. This is the screen ___________ the TV.
6. Judy and Ken have a big house. The big house is _________ .
7. My school ______ name is ABC primary school.
8. We have some mobile phones. These are ___________ mobile phones.
9. Henry has a dog. ___________ name is Frankie.
10. That is the bird's nest. The nest is _________ .

chapter 8

不指定冠詞：a和an

Articles: Indefinite article “a” and “an”

媽媽帶安安去逛百貨公司，安安跟媽媽說：「I want a toy.」（我想要一件玩具。）媽媽問她想要哪一件玩具，安安只是不斷重複地說：「I want a toy. I want a toy.」（我想要一件玩具。我想要一件玩具。）媽媽仍攪不懂到底安安想要哪一件玩具。

大家有沒有發現安安所說的話，使用了冠詞（Articles）中的不定冠詞（Indefinite article），即「a」？到底甚麼是冠詞呢？冠詞必須放在名詞前面，不能單獨使用，通常用來幫助說明名詞（Nouns）。冠詞一般可分為不定冠詞（Indefinite article）和定冠詞（Definite article）。本篇主要講解不定冠詞。

a和an的用法

不定冠詞（Indefinite article），即「a」和「an」，通常用於單數可數名詞前面，即「a/an＋名詞」，表示「一」的意義，但不強調數量，常用於**泛指某一類人、事或物，以及泛指某人或某物，但沒有具體指明是甚麼人或哪件物品。**例如：「a toy」（一件玩具）、「a baby」（一個嬰兒）、「an orange」（一個橙）、「an egg」（一個雞蛋），等等。這些例子都說明事物只有一個/件，但沒有特別指明是哪一個/件。大家看看這個句子：Johnny has a book.（尊尼有一本書。）

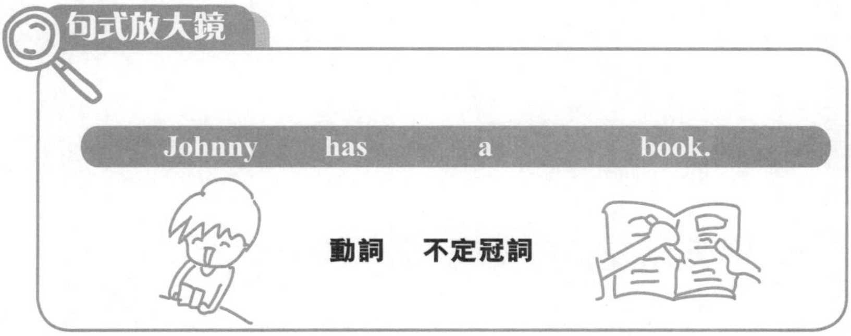

在「Johnny has a book.」這個句子裡，它只說明Johnny有一本書，但到底是哪一本呢？我們不知道，因為句子只說有一本書，沒有指明是哪一本。

我們怎樣決定某個名詞前面用「a」或「an」呢？一般來說，「a」用於輔音開頭的名詞前面，如「a boy」（一個男孩）、「a university」（一間大學）、「a chair」（一張椅子），等等。「an」用於元音開頭的名詞前面，如「an hour」（一小時）、「an island」（一個島）、「an elephant」（一隻象）、「an umbrella」（一把傘），等等。

8 Articles: Indefinite article "a" and "an"

文法加油站

練習一

請為以下名詞加上正確的不定冠詞。

1. ________ egg
2. ________ doctor
3. ________ pig
4. ________ supermarket
5. ________ ink
6. ________ bottle
7. ________ bus
8. ________ bird
9. ________ animal
10. ________ box

練習二

請圈出正確的答案。

1. I have (a / an) cup.
2. This is (a / an) orange.
3. She has (a / an) book.
4. Mr. Lee owns (a / an) shop
5. There is (a / an) office.
6. There is (a / an) university.
7. We have (a / an) hour for the examination.
8. This is (a / an) table.
9. This is (a / an) island.
10. There is (a / an) elephant.

挑戰站

參看例子，在正確的位置上加上「a」或「an」。

例子：Kitty has book.

Kitty has ^a book.

1. There is apple on the table.
2. Cup is on the book shelf.
3. I have orange.
4. There is university in Shatin.
5. You have hour to do homework.
6. There is elephant in the zoo.
7. Boy is standing under the tree.
8. There is girl in the classroom.
9. Book is under the chair.
10. There is umbrella in the basket.

chapter 9

指定冠詞：the

Articles: Definite article "the"

安安一直在百貨公司哭鬧，媽媽問她想要哪一件玩具，安安最後跟媽媽說：「I want the toy.」（我想要那件玩具。），一邊說，一邊指着一個小女孩手中的玩具。媽媽最後雖然知道安安想要哪一件玩具，但是媽媽說：「The toy was sold out.」（那件玩具已經賣完了。）

大家有沒有發現安安和媽媽所說的話，都使用了冠詞（Articles）中的定冠詞（Definite article），即「the」。

9 Articles: Definite article "the"

the特指某人或某物

定冠詞（Definite article），即「the」，常置於名詞前面，即「the ＋名詞」，用來表示名詞為特定的、指明的，具有「這」、「那」、「這些」、「那些」的含意。一般來說，名詞前面有定冠詞「the」，可以表示以下意義：

(1) 特指某（些）人或某（些）事物，例如：

Kelly wants the book.

嘉莉想要那本書。

Daddy is making the car model.

爸爸正在做那個模型車。

(2) 指談話雙方都知道的人或事物，例如：

Please open the door.

請打開那個門。

See you at the shop.

在那間商店見。

(3) 上文曾提及的人或事物，例如：

She has a bag. The bag is yellow.

她有一個書包。那書包是黃色的。

I have a house. The house is expensive.

我有一間屋。那間屋是昂貴的。

(4) 世界上獨一無二的事物，例如：

The sun is bigger than the earth.

太陽比地球大。

The moon is round tonight.

今晚月亮是圓的。

大家看看以下句子：

The house is mine.

那間屋是我的。

句式放大鏡

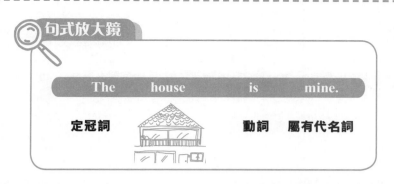

The	house	is	mine.
定冠詞		動詞	屬有代名詞

在「The house is mine.」這個句子裡，由於名詞「house」前面有「the」，因此，它不是説任何一間屋，而是説話人特指的那間屋。其他例子有：「the boy」（這/那個男孩）、「the book」（這/那本書）、「the man」（這/那個男人）、「the cup」（這/那個杯子），等等。

大家要留意，有些名詞前面加上或沒有加上「the」會有不同的意義。

名詞前面沒有「the」	名詞前面加上「the」
in hospital　住院	in the hospital　在醫院裡
go to sea　出海	go to the sea　去海邊
at table　進餐	at the table　在桌子旁
by sea　乘船	by the sea　在海邊
go to school　上學	go to the school　到學校
on horseback　騎着馬	on the horseback　在馬背上

文法加油站

練習一

請圈出正確的答案。

1. (X / The) house is hers.
2. I go to (X / the) school by bus.
3. Today is parent’s day. Richard is going to (X / the) school with his parent.
4. (X / The) watch is Mr. Wong’s.
5. I lost my pen. (X / The) pen is my birthday present.
6. Sue is looking for her shoes. (X / The) shoes are red.
7. Have you played (X / the) game?
8. Did you read (X / the) book? It is very interesting.
9. Who is (X / the) tall boy?
10. Where is (X / the) cat?

挑戰站

請填上正確的冠詞 (a, an , the)，如果無需加冠詞，請畫上×。

1. He gave Sally ______ useful book yesterday.

2. Francis is ______ honest boy.

3. There is _____ apple on the table.

4. The girl under ______ tree is my sister.

5. Anna comes from ______ USA.

6. This is _____ film I have seen.

7. ________ sun is shining.

8. There are many animals in _____ earth.

9. I am reading _____ book.

10. I like _____ picture on the wall.

11. _____ boy wearing glasses is my friend. His name is Chris.

12. ______ yellow flowers are on the table.

13. This is _____ book I have read.

14. ______ moon is bright tonight.

15. Judy is ______ smart girl.

16. Ken is ______ most hardworking student in the class.

17. _____ man talking to my mommy is my teacher.

18. I will make _____ cheese cake for your birthday.

19. _____ train will depart at 10:00PM.

20. I have seen _____ pencil box in the classroom.

chapter 10

認識三類動詞：

Verbs: Verb-to-be, Verb-to-have and Verb-to-do

丁丁和嘉嘉玩「動詞蓋棉被」遊戲，誰會勝出呢？丁丁有一張動詞卡，上面寫着「do」，並把它打出來，嘉嘉手頭上有「I」主詞卡，於是馬上打出來。輪到嘉嘉把「does」動詞卡打出來後，丁丁接着打出「We」主詞卡，結果丁丁輸了，要罰抽兩張動詞卡。

丁丁為甚麼輸了呢？因為他沒有考慮到主詞與動詞變化的關係。到底甚麼是動詞（Verbs）呢？動詞是表示動作、狀況或感覺，如「stand」（站立）、「cry」（哭）、「run」（跑）等等，都是動詞。大家猜猜下列句子，哪句是表示動作？哪句是表示狀況？哪句是表示感覺？

I clean the room.（我打掃房間。） ➪ 表示動作

I am a doctor.（我是醫生。） ➪ 表示狀況

I feel hot.（我覺得熱。） ➪ 表示感覺

Verb-to-be

英語動詞基本上可分為「Verb-to-be」、「Verb-to-have」和「Verb-to-do」三類，**需因應主詞（Subject）的不同而使用不同的動詞**，例如主詞是「She」，「Verb-to-be」動詞就是「is」、「Verb-to-have」動詞就是「has」和「Verb-to-do」動詞就是「does」。

「Verb-to-be」即以「be」作動詞基本形，按主詞的不同而使用「am」、「is」、「are」的其中一個。大家需緊記以下主詞和「Verb-to-be」動詞變化關係表：

		主詞	動詞基本形	Verb-to-be動詞
第一身	單數	I（我）	be（是）	am
	複數	We（我們）		are
第二身	單數	You（你）		are
	複數	You（你們）		are
第三身	單數	He（他）		is
		She（她）		is
		It（牠/它）		is
	複數	They（他們）		are

例子：

I am Kelly.
我是嘉莉。

We are pupils.
我們是小學生。

You are happy.
你/你們是快樂的。

They are sisters.
她們是姐妹。

He is a doctor.
他是一個醫生。

She is a teacher.
她是一個老師。

It is big.
牠/它是大的。

Verb-to-have

「Verb-to-have」即以「have」作動詞基本形，按主詞的不同而使用「have」、「has」的其中一個。大家看看以下主詞和「Verb-to-have」動詞變化關係表：

例子：

I have a book.
我有一本書。

We have a house.
我們有一所房子。

You have a sister.
你/你們有一個姐姐。

They have a red car.
他們有一輛紅色的車。

He has some pens.
他有一些筆。

She has a doll.
她有一個玩偶。

It has a tail.
牠有一條尾巴。

		主詞	動詞基本形	Verb-to-have動詞
第一身	單數	I (我)	have (有)	have
	複數	We (我們)		have
第二身	單數	You (你)		have
	複數	You (你們)		have
第三身	單數	He (他)		has
		She (她)		has
		It (牠/它)		has
	複數	They (他們)		have

Verb-to-do

「Verb-to-do」即以「do」作動詞基本形，按主詞的不同而使用「do」、「does」的其中一個。大家緊記以下主詞和「Verb-to-do」動詞變化關係表：

		主詞	動詞基本形	Verb-to-have動詞
第一身	單數	I (我)	do (有)	do
	複數	We (我們)		do
第二身	單數	You (你)		do
	複數	You (你們)		do
第三身	單數	He (他)		does
		She (她)		does
		It (牠/它)		does
	複數	They (他們)		do

例子：

I **do** homework.
我做功課。

We **do** exercises in the morning.
我們在早上做運動。

You **do** housework.
你/你們做家務。

They **do** homework.
他們做功課。

He **does** exercises in the morning.
他在早上做運動。

She **does** housework at night.
她晚上做家務。

10 Verbs: Verb-to-be,Verb-to-have and Verb-to-do

文法加油站

練習一

參看例子，圈出句中的動詞。

例子：These (are) my books.

1. Mommy is cleaning the room.
2. These are my friends.
3. Tracy borrowed the book from library.
4. Mr. Smith did exercises in the park.
5. Rabbits have long ears.
6. Grandpa lives in China.
7. Daddy bought me a new book.
8. Please sit down.
9. The children played football last week.
10. The cartoon is very interesting.

練習二

請圈出正確的答案。

1.They (do / does) homework at two o'clock.

2.He (am / is / are) my friend.

3.I (am / is / are) a teacher.

4.We (has / have) a big house.

5.You (am / is / are) a policemen.

6.The old man always (do / does) exercise in the morning.

7.May and Sue (do / does) housework every night.

8.Peter and Kitty (has / have) two children.

9.We (am / is / are) Chinese.

10.Frankie is my cat. It (has / have) a long tail.

挑戰站

請將正確的答案寫在橫線上。

1. Mommy always __________ housework after dinner.

2. Grandma and I __________ exercise in the park this morning.

3. Bobby _________a room. It's messy.

4. Chris _______ my brother. He's very tall.

5. Gordon and Danny ___________ good friends.

6. Kitty and Amy ___________ in the same class.

7. I _________ some toys.

8. I ___________ six years old.

9. It__________ my dog. Its name is Danny.

10. She_________ two sisters.

chapter 11

動詞的現在、過去和將來

Verbs: Tense

丁丁和嘉嘉玩「動詞變變變」遊戲，誰會勝出呢？丁丁抽了一張動詞卡，上面寫着「play」，然後抽了一張主詞卡「Tom and Karen」和一張時間卡「Yesterday」。丁丁要決定手中的動詞是否需要變動，他把動詞「play」改成「played」。他答對了！得10分。嘉嘉抽到「eat」動詞卡、「He」主詞卡和「Today」時間卡，她決定不改變動詞，結果她輸了。大家知道是甚麼原因嗎？

嘉嘉輸了是因為她沒有把動詞「eat」變為「eats」。為甚麼要在「eat」的尾部加「s」呢？那是因為動詞（Verbs）受到主詞和時態（Tense）的影響。

甚麼是時態？

我們在描述事情時，通常都會**說出事情發生時的時間**，這在英語中稱為時態（Tense）。時態會影響句子中的動詞，例如過去式（Past　Tense）的時態，動詞就要用過去式；現在式（Present　Tense）的時態，動詞就要用現在式；將來式（Future Tense）的時態，動詞就要用將來式。大家看看以下時間線圖：

Last year Kelly was five years old.
去年嘉莉是五歲。

This year Kelly is six years old.
今年嘉莉是六歲。

Next year Kelly will be seven years old.
明年嘉莉是七歲。

句式放大鏡

	表示時間的字詞	主詞	動詞變化	所描述的事情。
過去式 ➩	Last year	Kelly	was	six years old.
現在式 ➩	This year	Kelly	is	seven years old.
將來式 ➩	Next Year	Kelly	will be	eight years old.

上面的三個句子分別表示過去、現在和將來三個不同的時態，句中的動詞要因應主詞和句子所表示的時間而變化。再看看以下時間線圖：

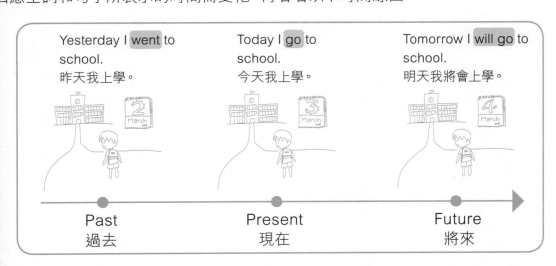

Yesterday I went to school.
昨天我上學。

Today I go to school.
今天我上學。

Tomorrow I will go to school.
明天我將會上學。

句式放大鏡

	表示時間的字詞	主詞	動詞變化	所描述的事情。
過去式 ➪	Yesterday	I	went	to school.
現在式 ➪	Today	I	go	to school.
將來式 ➪	Tomorrow	I	will go	to school.

上面的三個句子分別表示過去、現在和將來三個不同的時態，句中的動詞也要因應句子所表示的時間而變化。

文法加油站

練習一

Verbs	Yesterday	Today	Tomorrow
例子： eat (吃)	ate	eat	will eat
1. be		am, is, are	
2. have			
3. sing			
4. run			
5. go			
6. play			
7. talk			
8. join			
9. drink			
10. write			

練習二

請在現在式的句子上寫上P、過去式的句子上寫上PS、將來式的句子上寫上F。

1. I am ten years old. ____________
2. She will go to America next week. ____________
3. Mr. Fong went to China yesterday. ____________
4. Miss Lee is my teacher. ____________
5. You played football last Sunday. ____________
6. We will go to hiking next Saturday. ____________
7. Mrs. Cheung swims every morning. ____________
8. Cathy and Tommy were in the same class last year. ____________
9. Mandy and Stella wash dishes. ____________
10. It has red eyes and long ears. ____________

挑戰站

請將正確的答案寫在橫線上。

1. The boys __________ (play) football every Sunday.
2. Daddy ___________ (work) in America next year.
3. We _________ (move) to Shatin next month.
4. Sam and Amy ______ (go) to hiking last week.
5. Stella and Vicent __________ (be) in the same class a few years ago.
6. Mandy _______ (be) eleven years old last year.
7. They _______ (have) two houses in the past.
8. Billy ________ (do) homework at four o'clock every day.
9. I ______ (be) a singer.
10. Miss Fisher ________ (like) playing tennis.

chapter 12

不規則動詞：現在和過去式拼法不同

Verbs: Regular and Irregular Verbs

摩摩和哈利玩「動詞守規矩」遊戲，誰會勝出呢？摩摩抽了一張動詞卡，上面寫着「play」，哈利馬上打出「ed」卡，並大聲説出「play」是規則動詞。哈利答對了，得10分。哈利抽到「eat」，摩摩決定打出「ed」卡，結果他輸了，原來「eat」是不規則動詞，摩摩應該打出「不規則動詞」卡，並串出「ate」。

摩摩輸了是因為「eat」不是「規則動詞」(Regular verbs)，而是「不規則動詞」(Irregular verbs)。

大家先觀察以下兩個動詞變化表，看看能否找出當中的不同？

A		B	
現在式	過去式	現在式	過去式
cook（煮）	cooked	read（讀）	read
look（看）	looked	write（寫）	wrote
listen（聽）	listened	do（做）	did

在A動詞變化表和B動詞變化表中，動詞的變化有甚麼特點？其實，A動詞變化表中的動詞，它們的過去式都是在字詞的尾部加「ed」，而B動詞變化表中的動詞，它們的過去式有些跟現在式一樣，有些則各有不同的變化。

A動詞變化表中的動詞，我們稱為規則動詞；而B動詞變化表中的動詞，我們稱為不規則動詞。不規則動詞在英語中的數量也不少，平時多做練習，是可以幫助大家記住這些動詞的變化。以下是一些規則動詞和不規則動詞的例子：

規則動詞

	現在式	過去式	備註
A	play（玩）	played	在尾部加「ed」
	add（加上）	added	
	talk（説話）	talked	
B	live（住）	lived	在尾部加「d」
	care（關心）	cared	
	hope（希望）	hoped	
C	carry （攜帶）	carried	先把「y」轉作「i」，然後接「ed」
	cry（哭）	cried	
	study（學習）	studied	
D	drop（滴下）	dropped	先把「p」再寫一次，然後接「ed」
	stop（停止）	stopped	

不規則動詞

現在式	過去式
am / is /are（是）	was /were
has / have（有）	had
do（做）	did
begin（開始）	began
break（打破）	broke
buy（買）	bought
catch（捕捉）	caught
draw（畫）	drew
drive（駕駛）	drove
feel（感覺）	felt

基本上，規則動詞的過去式是直接在字詞的尾部加「ed」，如規則動詞表中的A類動詞。不過，大家要注意有些規則動詞的尾部是「e」，表示過去式時，只需在尾部直接加上「d」即可，如規則動詞表中的B類動詞。但是，也有一些尾部是「e」的動詞不能直接加上「d」，如「ride」（騎），這是因為「ride」是不規則動詞啊！

此外，如果動詞尾部最後一個字母是「y」，表示過去式時，就要先把「y」轉作「i」，然後才接「ed」，如規則動詞表中的C類動詞。另外，還有一些規則動詞尾部最後一個字母是「p」，表示過去式時，就要先把「p」再寫一次，然後才接「ed」，如規則動詞表中的D類動詞。

文法加油站

練習一

將句中的動詞圈出來，然後是規則動詞的，就在橫線上寫上「R」，不規則動詞的寫上「I」。

例子：She drew a picture. I

The baby cried loudly. R

1. Dick and Kenney were in the same class last year. ____
2. Amy went to school by MTR. ____
3. I did housework last night. ____
4. You played table tennis yesterday. ____
5. We had a big house in the past. ____
6. They visited their grandparent last month. ____
7. He was a fireman a few years ago. ____
8. She danced with Raymond in the party. ____
9. The weather was not good last week. ____
10. Peggy and Ray flew to Japan last night. ____

練習二

請將正確的答案寫在橫線上。

1. We _________ (visit) grandpa last week.
2. Kitty and Ray ______ (dance) in the party last night.
3. Mr. Lee _______ (be) a policeman last year.
4. They ________ (have) dinner last month.
5. Sue _______ (do) homework until 1:00AM last night.
6. I ________ (see) him running to the room yesterday.
7. Joe ________ (tell) me the story a few days ago.
8. Joanna _______ (come) late yesterday.
9. We _________ (talk) about it last week.
10. Somebody _________ (sing) a song last night.

挑戰站

請將正確的答案寫在橫線上。

現在式	過去式	現在式	過去式
1. sit	________	10. feel	________
2. run	________	11. build	________
3. read	________	12. show	________
4. listen	________	13. ride	________
5. speak	________	14. put	________
6. swim	________	15. wear	________
7. think	________	16. cut	________
8. eat	________	17. see	________
9. give	________	18. go	________

chapter 13

動名詞：動詞當名詞用

Verbals: Gerunds

爸爸媽媽帶小茜上街去，爸爸問小茜要不要吃芝士蛋糕，小茜說：「I dislike eating cheese cake.」（我不喜歡吃芝士蛋糕。）後來，媽媽問小茜要不要吃冰淇淋，小茜開心地說：「I like eating ice cream.」（我喜歡吃冰淇淋。）

小茜回答父母時所說的話，都包含了動狀詞（Verbals）中的動名詞（Gerunds）。動狀詞（Verbals）可以是動名詞（Gerunds）或不定詞（Infinitives）。這一章主要講解動名詞（Gerunds）。

甚麼是動名詞？

在英語語法裡，由於一個句子只能有一個動詞（Verbs），因此，如句子需要同時用上另一個動詞，就要把這個動詞以動名詞的形式表現出來。例如「I dislike eating cheese cake.」一句，「dislike」是動詞，「eating」是動名詞。動名詞主要由「動詞基本形＋ing」組成，在句子裡通常作為名詞來使用。例如：「I like drinking tea.」（我喜歡喝茶。）「We enjoy reading.」（我們享受閱讀。）等等。

句式放大鏡

We	enjoy	reading.
	**動詞**	**動詞基本形+ing**

在「We enjoy reading.」這個句子裡，「enjoy」是動詞，「reading」作為動名詞，所表示的是閱讀這項活動，而不是閱讀的動作。再看看其他例子：

Sally likes cooking.
莎莉喜歡烹飪。

They are good at singing.
他們擅長唱歌。

動名詞與動詞的分別

動名詞與動詞有甚麼分別呢？大家比較以下句子：

A. Sally cooks every day.
莎莉每天都煮食。

B. Sally likes cooking.
莎莉喜歡烹飪。

在A句子裡，「cook」是動詞；在B句子裡，「like」是動詞，「cook」只能以「動詞基本形＋ing」的動名詞形式出現，成為名詞。因此，在B句子裡，「cooking」所表達的是烹飪這個活動，而不是煮食的動作。

大家要留意，以下這些動詞後面如再接另一個動詞，通常都要加「ing」。

enjoy（享受）	mind（介意）	stop（停止）	finish（完成）
like（喜歡）	consider（考慮）	miss（錯失）	deny（否認）
dislike（不喜歡）	suggest（建議）	keep（不斷）	admit（承認）

例子：

I will consider working in France.
我會考慮在法國工作。

She suggested going to Lamma Island.
她提議去南丫島。

Please stop shouting.
請停止叫喊。

文法加油站

練習一

請圈出句中的動名詞，並在動詞下加橫線。

1. She dislikes swimming.
2. Kelly and Amy begin crying.
3. Please stop talking.
4. He likes smoking.
5. I hate doing homework.
6. Alice and Tim enjoy singing.
7. He suggests going to China.
8. Please keep doing exercise.
9. Michael likes cooking.
10. Judy dislikes making models.

練習二

請圈出正確的答案。

1. I will consider (stayed / to stay / staying) one more day in Japan.
2. We dislike (had / to have / having) barbecue.
3. Alan and Kitty enjoy (swam / to swim / swimming).
4. Ivan promised (buy / to buy / buying) Sandy a new watch.
5. Jackson denied (broke / to break / breaking) the vase.
6. Tommy suggests (went / to go / going) to Lamma Island this Sunday.
7. The pandas like (eat / to eat / eating) bamboo.
8. I keep (thought / to think / thinking) the question.
9. I like (made / to make / making) models.
10. Alice enjoys (play / to play / playing) piano.

挑戰站

請圈出句中的錯誤，並將正確的答案寫在右面的橫線上。

1. Daddy dislikes keep fit. ____________
2. Please stop run. ____________
3. You should keep do exercises. ____________
4. Mandy enjoys read. ____________
5. Mike likes drink tea. ____________
6. You promised give me the book. ____________
7. Uncle Peter will consider work in Japan. ____________
8. The dog begins eat. ____________
9. The baby stop cry. ____________

chapter 14

不定詞：to＋動詞基本形

Verbals: Infinitives

小茜和爸爸媽媽去逛商場，小茜看到一個可愛的布偶玩具，就向媽媽撒嬌說：「I want to buy the doll.」（我想買這個布偶。）媽媽不想小茜養成隨意買東西的壞習慣，不准她買布偶玩具。小茜於是一邊哭，一邊說：「I want to have a new mommy.」（我想有一個新媽媽。）令爸爸和媽媽哭笑不得。

小茜所說的話包含了不定詞（Infinitives），如「to have」、「to buy」。在英語語法裡，由於一個句子只能有一個動詞（Verbs），因此，如句子同時有另一個動作，就要把這個動詞以動名詞或不定詞的形式表現出來。例如 「I want to buy the doll.」一句，「want」是動詞，「to buy」是不定詞。

to不定詞

不定詞可用作名詞、形容詞或副詞，它可分為有「to」的不定詞 (To infinitives) 和沒有「to」的不定詞 (Bare infinitives)。

「To」不定詞的形式是「to＋動詞基本形」，如「to see」(看)、「to drink」(喝)，等等。大家看看以下句子：

Daddy promises <u>to buy</u> me a toy car.
爸爸答應買一架玩具車給我。

句式放大鏡

Daddy	promises	to buy	me	a toy car.
	動詞	to＋動詞基本形	人物代名詞	

在「Daddy promises to buy me a toy car.」這個句子裡，動詞是「promise」，「to」不定詞是「to buy」。再看看其他例子：

She wants to buy a computer.
她想買一台電腦。

Amy and Judy plan to travel China.
艾美和茱迪計劃去中國旅遊。

大家要留意，以下這些動詞後面如再接另一個動詞，通常都要使用「to＋動詞基本形」（即「To不定詞」）。

need（需要）	promise（答應）	plan（計劃）
want（想/希望）	learn（學習）	intend（打算）
agree（同意）	decide（決定）	expect（期望）

再看看以下例子：

I need something to drink.
我需要喝一些東西。

Mary agrees to join the singing team.
瑪利同意參加那個歌唱組。

Uncle Danny decides to work in America.
丹尼叔叔決定在美國工作。

沒有to的不定詞

沒有「to」不定詞的形式其實就是沒有「To」的動詞基本形，通常句中出現某些動詞，如「make」（弄/令到）、「let」（讓）、「help」（幫助），以及一些感覺動詞，如「hear」（聽）、「feel」（感覺）、「watch」（看）、「see」（看）等，則動詞後面無需使用「to＋動詞基本形」，而只需使用動詞基本形即可。大家看看以下句子：

Jack makes his brother cry.
積克令他的弟弟哭。

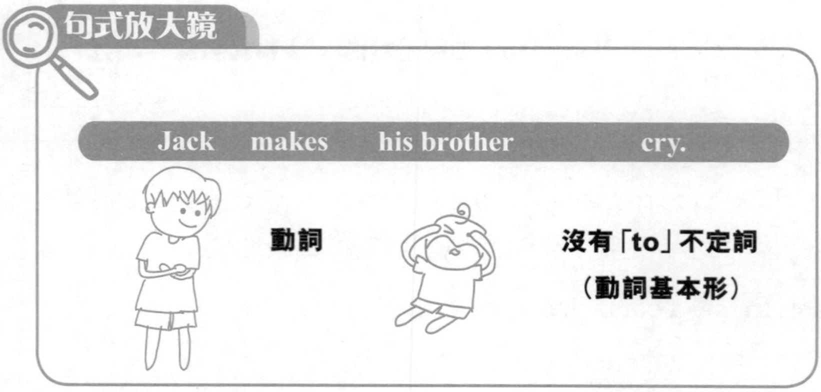

在「Jack makes his brother cry.」這個句子裡，動詞是「make」，沒有「to」不定詞是「cry」。再看看其他例子：

Please let me know.	請讓我知道。
Sam helps Peter solve the Maths problem.	森姆幫彼德解決那個數學難題。
I saw Tony run to post office.	我看見東尼跑去郵政局。

句中如出現以下動詞，則另一個動詞可以使用動名詞（Gerunds）或不定詞（Infinitives），意思是一樣的：

remember（記起）	love（喜愛）	try（嘗試）
like（喜歡）	hate（討厭）	begin（開始）

例如：

The baby begins to cry. The baby begins crying.	那個嬰兒開始哭。
I love to swim. I love swimming.	我喜愛游泳。

文法加油站

練習一

參看例子，將句中的動詞畫底線，將「to」不定詞和沒有「to」不定詞圈出來。

例子：I need (to go) now.

Please help me (make) the model.

1. I need to drink something.
2. Hong Kong people love to eat Japanese food.
3. Johnny agrees to go hiking with us.
4. Kerry needs to do homework at four o'clock.
5. Please let me know what happened.
6. The fat man should begin to keep fit now.
7. I try to see you this weekend.
8. Kitty hates to do homework.
9. Mr. Wong wants to buy a new computer.
10. Mandy helps her child to wash hair.

練習二

請圈出正確的答案。

1. Would you let me (see / to see / seeing) your bag?
2. We expect our grandparent (arrive / to arrive / arriving) tomorrow.
3. Alan and Sam have learned (swim / to swim / swimming) this summer holidays.
4. Ivan wants (buy / to buy / buying) this watch.
5. I need (go / to go / going) now.
6. Tammy agrees (go / to go / going) to Sai Kung this Sunday.
7. Please let me (know / knew / knowing) what happened.
8. Let me (tell / to tell / telling) you the truth.
9. I am hungry. I need something (eat / to eat / eating).
10. Alice helps her mother (wash / to wash / playing) dishes.

挑戰站

請將正確的動狀詞答案寫在橫線上。

1. Let me ____________ (show) you the way.
2. Amy dislikes ______________ (play) piano.
3. Do you like ______________ (make) model?
4. Greg is good at ____________ (draw).
5. Sandy saw Tommy _________ (rush) to the bus stop.
6. ____________ (swim) can improve our body.
7. I am pleased ________ (meet) you.
8. The children denied _________ (break) the vase.
9. Daddy suggests __________ (visit) grandma on Sunday.
10. Ray plans __________ (study) in Canada.

chapter 15

形容詞

描述形容詞、數量和所屬者

Adjectives: Descriptive, Quantity and Demonstrative

老師帶小華和同學們參觀嘉道理農場。農場裡，有很多動物和植物。小華說：「A fat pig.」（一隻胖胖的豬。）佩佩說：「A cute chicken.」（一隻可愛的小雞。）安琪說：「This apple tree is tall.」（這蘋果樹高高的。）盈盈高聲呼叫說：「What a beautiful flower!」（這花很漂亮啊！）

大家有沒有留意，上面的小朋友在描述農場裡的事物時，都使用了形容詞（Adjectives）。形容詞是**用來描述各種事物的詞語**，如「fat」（胖的）、「tall」（高的）、「cute」（可愛的）、「beautiful」（漂亮的），等等。

形容詞通常放在名詞（Nouns）前面，即「形容詞＋名詞」，用來修飾或指出名詞，如「a tall man」（高的男人）、「a lovely dog」（可愛的狗）、「a beautiful hat」（漂亮的帽子），等等。

形容詞的分類

形容詞可為描述形容詞（Descriptive Adjectives）、數量形容詞（Adjectives of Quantity）、屬有形容詞（Possessive Adjectives）、指示形容詞（Demonstrative Adjectives）等。

(1) 描述形容詞主要用來描述名詞，如：「young」（年輕的）、「old」（年老的）、「happy」（開心的）、「sad」（憂愁的）等等。

(2) 數量形容詞主要用來描述事物（或名詞）的數量、次序等，如：「one」（一）、「ten」（十）、「many」（很多）、「few」（很少）、「first」（第一）、「fifth」（第五），等等。

(3) 屬有形容詞主要用來描述事物（或名詞）由誰人或甚麼物所擁有，如「my」（我的）、「his」（他的）、「theirs」（他們的）、「its」（牠/它的），等等。

(4) 指示形容詞主要有四個，通常用來指出名詞，如「this」（這個）、「that」（那個）、「these」（這些）、「those」（那些）。

以下句子中的形容詞，屬於哪一類呢？

Bobby is a big dog.（波比是一隻大狗。）
She lives in a small house.（她住在一間小的屋子。）
⇨描述形容詞

She has one book.（她有一本書。）
The first month is January.（第一個月份是一月。）
⇨數量形容詞

This is my house.（這是我的房子。）
Her name is Joey.（她的名子是祖兒。）
⇨屬有形容詞

This cat is lovely.（這隻貓是可愛的。）
Those books belong to Jack.（那些書是屬於積克的。）
⇨指示形容詞

形容詞獨特的「尾巴」

大家或會擔心，英文詞語這麼多，怎樣才能分辨哪個是形容詞呢？其實，大家只要細心觀察不同的形容詞，就會發現它們有一些特別的「尾巴」，通常形容詞的結尾都由「-ent」、「-al」、「-ous」、「-ive」、「-ful」、「-able」、「-ish」和「-less」組成。大家看看下表：

結尾	例子
以「-ent」結尾	existent（存在的）
	different（不同的）
以「-al」結尾	national（國家的）
	historical（歷史的）
以「-ous」結尾	dangerous（危險的）
	continuous（持續的）
以「-ive」結尾	active（積極的）
	attractive（具吸引力的）
以「-ful」結尾	careful（小心的）
	beautiful（美麗的）
以「-able」結尾	comfortable（舒服的）
	enjoyable（享受的）
以「-ish」結尾	foolish（愚笨的）
	selfish（自私的）
以「-less」結尾	careless（不小心的）
	useless（無用的）

我們描述事物時，有時會用兩個或以上的形容詞來形容。如果一個名詞有多於一個形容詞時，通常形容詞的排列次序是：「意見形容詞（Optional adjectives）＋事實形容詞（Factual adjectives）＋名詞（Nouns）」。意見形容詞通常是個人對事物的主觀描述，而事實形容詞則是根據客觀事實來描述事物。例如：

This is an expensive wooden table.（這是一張昂貴的木質桌子）

意見形容詞　事實形容詞

Simon is a hardworking Chinese doctor.（西門是一位勤奮的中國醫生。）

意見形容詞　事實形容詞

文法加油站

練習一

請為下列詞語加上適當的結尾，使它成為形容詞。

-ent -al -ous -ive -ful -able -ish -less

1. child ______
2. care ______
3. fame ______
4. fool ______
5. beauty ______
6. use ______
7. book ______
8. enjoy ______
9. value ______
10. depend ______
11. music ______
12. differ ______
13. nation ______
14. create ______
15. act ______

練習二

請圈出句中的形容詞。

1. I have three cars.
2. This is his watch.
3. It's an expensive watch.
4. This dog is hers.
5. The last month is December.
6. Grandpa lives in a big house.
7. Snow White is beautiful.
8. Alex has many books.
9. Those boys like playing football.
10. His teacher is Mr. Wong.

挑戰站

請圈出句中的形容詞，並判斷它的類別，將代號寫在右方。

描述形容詞（AQ） 數量形容詞（AQy） 屬有形容詞（PA） 指示形容詞（DA）

1. David has one sister. ________
2. These are my toys. ________
3. It's an interesting film. ________
4. Those books are theirs. ________
5. The first season is spring. ________
6. We live in a beautiful house. ________
7. Johnny is a smart boy. ________
8. Faye has some milk in the morning. ________
9. These girls like singing. ________
10. Our teacher is Miss Lee. ________

chapter 16

比較級的形容詞

Adjectives: Comparative form of adjectives

小華和同學們在嘉道理農場看到很多有趣的事物。小華說：「This pig is fatter than that one.」（這隻豬比那隻更胖。）佩佩說：「The chicken is smaller than the hen.」（那隻小雞比母雞更小。）安琪說：「This apple tree is taller than the mango tree.」（這棵蘋果樹比那棵芒果樹更高。）。

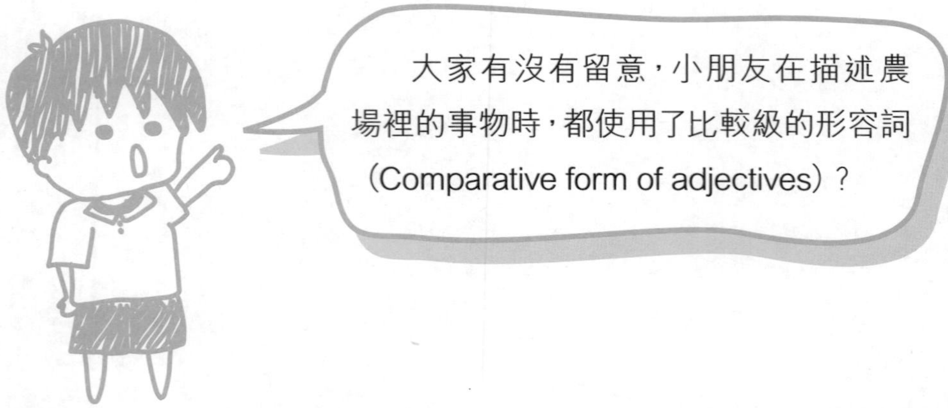
大家有沒有留意，小朋友在描述農場裡的事物時，都使用了比較級的形容詞（Comparative form of adjectives）？

甚麼是比較級的形容詞？

形容詞除了用來描述事物外，也可以**用來比較兩個或以上的事物，從中分出級別，**我們可稱它為比較級的形容詞（Comparative form of adjectives）。

一般來說，形容詞可分為三種級別，即原級（Positive form）、比較級（Comparative form）和最高級（Superlative form）。當形容詞要作不同級別的比較時，通常會把形容詞原級作一定形式的變化，大家可參看下表：

形容詞原級（Positive form）	形容詞比較級（Comparative form）	形容詞最高級（Superlative form）
單音節形容詞： 比較級在結尾加「-er」、最高級在結尾加「-est」		
clean（乾淨的） short（短/矮的）	cleaner（更乾淨的） shorter（更短/矮的）	cleanest（最乾淨的） shortest（最短/矮的）
單音節及短響音形容詞： 如最後的字母是「d」、「g」、「m」、「n」和「t」， 比較級在重複最後的字母後加「-er」、 最高級在重複最後的字母後結尾加「-est」		
big（大的） fat（胖的）	bigger（更大的） fatter（更胖的）	biggest（最大的） fattest（最胖的）
雙音節形容詞： 如結尾是「y」，比較級先把「y」改為「-i」然後接「-er」、 最高級也是先把「y」改為「-i」然後接「-est」		
happy（快樂的） funny（有趣的）	happier（更快樂的） funnier（更有趣的）	happiest（最快樂的） funniest（最有趣的）
三音節以上的形容詞： 比較級是「more＋形容詞原級＋than」、 最高級是「the＋ most＋形容詞原級」		
interesting（有趣的）beautiful（漂亮的）	more interesting than（更有趣的） more beautiful than（更漂亮的）	the most interesting（最有趣的） the most beautiful（最漂亮的）

16 Adjectives: Comparative form of adjectives

原級

原級(Positive form)是指形容詞原來的級別，沒有比較的含意，如「She has a beautiful dress.」(她有一條漂亮的裙子。)，以及用來表示兩個事物的質量是相同的，通常會使用「as＋形容詞＋as」來表達，如「Amy's dress is as beautiful as Stella's.」(艾美的裙子和斯特拉的一樣漂亮。)

句式放大鏡

She	has	a	beautiful	dress.
	動詞	冠詞	形容詞原級	

Amy's dress	is	as beautiful as	Stella's.
	動詞	as＋形容詞原級＋as	

上面兩個句子都使用了形容詞原級，卻用了不同的表達方式。在「She has a beautiful dress.」這個句子裡，句中使用了形容詞原級，即「beautiful」來表達裙子是漂亮的。而在「Amy's dress is as beautiful as Stella's.」這個句子裡，句中使用了「as＋形容詞＋as」來表示艾美和斯特拉的裙子都一樣漂亮。再看看其他例子：

Daddy has a bad headache.
爸爸有嚴重的頭痛。

The weather is good.
天氣好。

This house is as big as his.
這間屋和他的一樣大。

Sally is as tall as Amy.
莎莉和艾美一樣高。

Bobby is as fat as Kenny.
波比和肯尼一樣胖。

比較級

比較級（Comparative form）是用來比較兩個質量不同的事物，常用的表達方式是「形容詞比較級＋than」，如「John is taller than Peter.」（約翰比彼得更高。），以及「more＋形容詞原級＋than」，如「Mandy is more beautiful than Stella.」（曼迪比斯特拉更漂亮。）

句式放大鏡
John is taller than Peter.
動詞
形容詞比較級＋than
Mandy is more beautiful than Stella.
動詞
more+形容詞原級＋than

上面的兩個句子，是形容詞作比較時兩種常見的表達方式，即「形容詞比較級＋than」和「more＋形容詞原級＋than」。在「John is taller than Peter.」這個句子裡，使用了「形容詞比較級＋than」來表示約翰比彼得更高。大家要留意，形容詞「tall」的結尾加了「er」，這是形容詞比較級常見的表達形式。

而「Mandy is more beautiful than Stella.」一句，句中使用了「more＋形容詞原級＋than」來表示曼迪比斯特拉更漂亮。為甚麼要把「more」放在形容詞「beautiful」前面呢？這是因為「beautiful」是三音節以上的形容詞。再看看其他例子：

My dog is bigger than your dog.
我的狗比你的狗更大。

He is fatter than you.
他比你更胖。

This book is more interesting than that book.
這本書比那本書更有趣。

She is more hardworking than you.
她比你更用功。

最高級

最高級 (Superlative form) 是用來比較三個或以上質量不同的事物，常用的表達方式是「the＋形容詞最高級」，如「He is the tallest boy in my class.」（他是我班最高的男孩。）以及「the＋most＋形容詞原級」，如「She is the most beautiful girl in my class.」（她是我班最漂亮的女孩。）

句式放大鏡

He	is	the tallest boy	in my class.
	動詞	the＋形容詞最高級	

She	is	the most beautiful girl	in my class.
	動詞	the+most+形容詞原級	

上面兩個句子是形容詞最高級作比較時兩種常見的表達方式，即「the＋形容詞最高級」和「the＋most＋形容詞原級」。在「He is the tallest boy in my class.」這個句子裡，句中使用了「the＋形容詞最高級」來表示在班中眾多男孩子之中，他是最高的。大家要留意，句中的形容詞最高級是在形容詞原級「tall」的結尾加「est」。而「She is the most beautiful girl in my class.」一句，使用了「the＋most＋形容詞原級」來表示在班中眾多女孩子之中，她是最漂亮的。再看看其他例子：

Sam is the bravest fireman in Hong Kong.
山姆是香港最勇敢的消防員。

This building is the oldest one in China.
這座建築物是中國最古老的。

Joyce is the most hardworking girl in my class.
喬依斯是我班最用功的女孩。

This watch is the most expensive item in this shop.
這錶是這間店最貴的物品。

最後，大家要注意，有小部分形容詞的比較級和最高級跟原級有很大的不同，包括：

原級（Positive form）	比較級（Comparative form）	最高級（Superlative form）
good（好的）	better（更好的）	the best（最好的）
bad（差/壞的）	worse（更差/壞的）	the worst（最差/壞的）
many（多的）	more（更多的）	most（最多的）
much（多的）	more（更多的）	most（最多的）
little（少的）	less（更少的）	least（最少的）

文法加油站

練習一

請寫出各級別的形容詞。

原級(Positive form)	比較級 (Comparative form)	最高級 (Superlative form)
1. careful		
2.	more hardworking	
3. interesting		
4. pretty		
5. hot		
6.	colder	
7. cheap		
8. expensive		
9. fat		
10. sad		
11.		the best
12. bad		
13. many		
14.	more	
15. little		

練習二

請圈出句中的形容詞，並判斷它的級別。

原級 (P)　比較級 (C)　最高級 (S)

1. David is smarter than Peter. ____________
2. This house is as beautiful as that house. ____________
3. It's a funny game. ____________
4. She is the most beautiful woman in the world. ____________
5. He is the laziest student in my class. ____________
6. I live in a small house. ____________
7. Johnny is a fat boy. ____________
8. Faye is the tallest girl in my school. ____________
9. Kitty is more hardworking than Danny. ____________
10. Miss Lee is the worst teacher in my school. ____________

挑戰站

請將正確的答案寫在橫線上。

1. This is the __________ (good) film this year.
2. I have _______________ (many) toys than you.
3. My bag is as ______________ (big) as hers.
4. The baby is _______________ (cute).
5. Grandpa is the___________________ (old) one in my family.
6. Miranda is _________________(short) than Sue.
7. Tammy is ___________ (helpful) than Peter.
8. Sammy is the ____________ (lazy) one in my class.
9. His car is _________________(expensive) than yours.
10. This dress is ______________ (bad) than that one.

chapter 17

副詞：經常做嗎？怎樣做？

Adverbs: Adverbs of Frequency and Manner

皓皓的朋友各有特點，他說：「Judy is a very clever girl.」（茱迪是一個很聰明的女孩。）「Tom always speak loudly.」（湯姆常常大聲地説話。）、「Alice is still talking on the phone.」（愛麗斯仍然在講電話。）......皓皓覺得跟這些各有特點的朋友相處，是一件有趣的事情。

大家有沒有留意，皓皓在描述他的朋友時，都使用了副詞（Adverbs）。副詞是用來修飾動詞（Verbs）或為動詞提供更多資訊的字詞，如「always」（總是/常常）、「loudly」（大聲地）、「still」（仍然），等等。另外，副詞也可以用來修飾形容詞（Adjectives），如「very clever」中的副詞「very」（很）是用來修飾形容詞「clever」（聰明的）。

副詞大致上可分為頻率副詞（Adverbs of Frequency）、方式副詞（Adverbs of Manner）、時間副詞（Adverbs of Time）、地方副詞（Adverbs of Place），以及程度副詞（Adverbs of Degree）。這一章主要講解頻率副詞和方式副詞。

17 Adverbs: Adverbs of Frequency and Manner

頻率副詞

頻率副詞主要用來描述事情發生的頻率，例如是否經常發生。大家要留意，頻率不等於次數。頻率副詞包括：「always」（總是/常常）、「sometimes」（有時）、「often」（經常）、「seldom」（很少）、「never」（從不）、「once」（曾經、一次）、「daily」（每天地）、「monthly」（每月地）、「regularly」（定期地）等，如「He always lies.」（他常常説謊。）

句式放大鏡

He always lies.

頻率副詞（always）　**動詞**（lies）

在「He always lies.」這個句子裡，動詞「lies」（説謊）前面使用了頻率副詞來進一步指出「説謊」的發生頻率。大家要留意副詞在句中的位置有時是放在動詞前面，有時是放在句末，要視乎句子的意思而定。其他例子有：

Sometimes grandpa wakes up at six o' clock.

有時祖父六時起床。

I never lie.

我從不説謊。

Tommy seldom contacts Lily.

湯米很少聯絡莉莉。

We go to cinema weekly.

我們每星期（地）去戲院。

方式副詞

方式副詞主要用來描述動作發生的方式，即怎樣做某事情。例如「loudly」（大聲地）、「happily」（快樂地）、「carefully」（小心地）、「carelessly」（不小心地）、「fast」（快速地）、「quickly」（快速地）、「busily」（忙碌地），等等，如「Miss Lee speaks softly to the students.」（李老師柔和地跟學生説話。）

句式放大鏡

Miss Lee speaks softly to the students.

動詞　方式副詞

在「Miss Lee speaks softly to the students.」這個句子裡，動詞「speaks」（說話）後面使用了方式副詞來進一步指出「說話」的發生方式。大家要留意副詞在句中的位置有時是放在動詞後面，有時是放在句末，要視乎句子的意思而定。其他例子有：

The children read quietly in the room.

孩子們在房間裡靜靜地閱讀。

They are busily doing homework.

他們正在忙碌地做功課。

I finished the car model easily.

我輕易地完成了這個汽車模型。

文法加油站

練習一

請圈出句中的副詞。

1. He broke the vase carelessly.
2. Grandpa always wakes up at six o'clock.
3. Nancy is busily doing homework.
4. Peter made the cheese cake easily.
5. I clean the vase carefully.
6. Amy speaks softly.
7. Karen seldom drinks coffee.
8. Andy sometimes goes to office by bus.
9. Mommy goes to supermarket weekly.
10. Joe and Alex never contact each other.

練習二

請將正確的答案寫在橫線上。

carelessly	quietly	softly	always	never
worse	clearly	loudly	carefully	suddenly

1. The baby cried ____________ last night.
2. She ______________ watches TV at midnight.
3. Amy broke the vase __________________ .
4. Miss Fong explains the question _______________ to us.
5. Grandpa is reading ______________ in his room.
6. Jeff __________ loses his stuff.
7. Tammy crosses the road ________________ .
8. Sunny and Rebecca sing ________________ .
9. His car broke down ______________ .
10. The weather is getting _________________ .

挑戰站

請圈出句中的副詞，並判斷它的類別。

頻率副詞（F）　方式副詞（M）

1. He walks slowly. ______
2. Grandma seldom watches TV after ten o'clock. ______
3. Nicky did homework carelessly. ______
4. I made the car model easily. ______
5. Mommy speaks softly. ______
6. Alex read quietly in his room. ______
7. Benson sometimes comes home late. ______
8. Andy sometimes goes to office by bus. ______
9. Miranda shouted suddenly. ______
10. Daddy goes to China monthly. ______

chapter 18

時間副詞、地方副詞和程度副詞

Adverbs: Adverbs of Time, Adverbs of Place and Adverbs of Degree

媽媽對皓皓說：「Grandpa and grandma will visit us tomorrow. Please tidy up your room and put the toys here.」（祖父和祖母明天會來探望我們。請你收拾房間，並把玩具放在這兒。）皓皓收拾好房間後，跟媽媽說：「I miss grandpa and grandma. I am very happy they will come.」（我掛念祖父和祖母。我很開心他們明天會來。）

皓皓和媽媽的對話，都使用了副詞（Adverbs）中的時間副詞（Adverbs of Time）（即「tomorrow」）、地方副詞（Adverbs of Place）（即「here」），以及程度副詞（Adverbs of Degree）（即「very」）。再次提一提大家，副詞是用來修飾動詞（Verbs）或為動詞提供更多資訊的字詞，以及可以用來修飾形容詞（Adjectives）。

時間副詞

時間副詞主要用來指出動作發生時的時間，即甚麼時候做某事情。例如「still」（仍然）、「already」（已經）、「today」（今天）、「yesterday」（昨天）、「tomorrow」（明天）、「ago」（之前）、「soon」（不久），等等，如「Daddy goes to China today.」（爸爸今天去中國。）

句式放大鏡

Daddy goes to China today.

goes：動詞　today：時間副詞

在「Daddy goes to China.」這個句子裡，句末出現了時間副詞「today」，用來說明動作（即動詞「goes」）發生的時間。大家要留意有些時間副詞會放在句末，有些則會放在動詞後面。其他例子有：

Uncle Sam will visit grandpa tomorrow .
湯姆叔叔明天將會探望祖父。

May was a policewoman three years ago .
三年前，美兒是一位女警。

I have already done my homework.
我已經做完了功課。

She is still drawing picture.
她仍然在畫畫。

地方副詞

地方副詞主要用來指出動作發生的地點，例如「everywhere」（四處）、「anywhere」（任何地方）、「there」（那裡）、「here」（這裡），等等，如「Alice puts the book here.」（愛麗斯把書放在這兒。）

句式放大鏡

Alice puts the book here.

puts：動詞　here：地方副詞

在「Alice puts the book here.」這個句子裡，句末出現的地方副詞「here」是用來說明動作（即動詞 「puts」）發生的地點。大家要留意地方副詞通常會放在句末。其他例子有：

Mommy can't find her watch anywhere .
媽媽在任何地方都找不到她的手錶。

Nancy is looking for her shoes everywhere
南茜正在四處尋找她的鞋子。

The library is there .
圖書館在那兒。

程度副詞

程度副詞主要用來加強或減弱動詞或形容詞所描述的程度，例如「just」(只是/僅僅)、「too」(過於)、「very」(非常)、「almost」(差不多)、「enough」(足夠)，等等，如「May just caught the train.」(美兒剛好趕上那火車。)、「Peter feels very happy.」(彼得覺得非常快樂。)

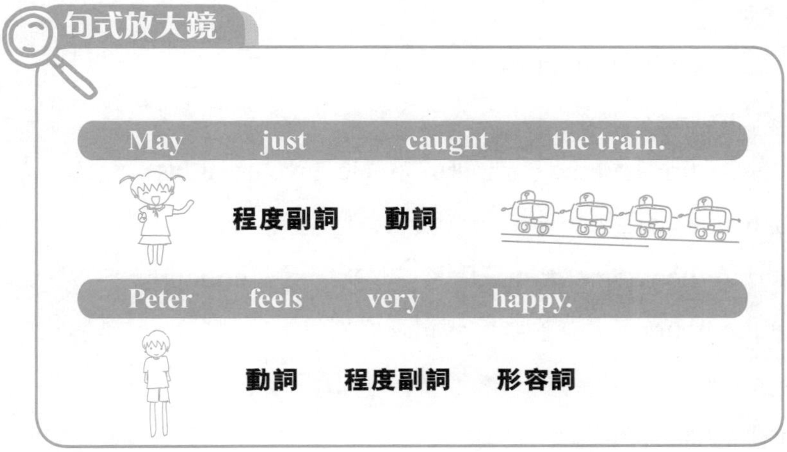

在「May just caught the train.」這個句子裡，程度副詞「just」在動詞「caught」前面，說明動作發生的程度只是剛剛好。而「Peter feels very happy.」一句，程度副詞「very」置於形容詞「happy」前面，說明所描述的心情的程度。其他例子有：

It's too hot today.(今天太熱了。)
The examination is quite difficult.(那個考試頗艱深。)
I almost lost the notebook.(我差點兒掉了那本筆記簿。)

文法加油站

練習一

請圈出句中的副詞。

1. It's very hot today.
2. Grandpa is looking for his glasses everywhere.
3. Please come here, David.
4. I did my homework a few hours ago.
5. The English test is quite difficult.
6. The oral examination is very easy.
7. I just finished the project.
8. Jack goes to school by MTR today.
9. Adrain always put his stuff everywhere.
10. Joey will go to Japan next month.

練習二

請填上正確的答案。

now	here	everywhere	still	ago
very	tomorrow	almost	too	there

1. Please put the box __________.
2. It was _______ cold last month.
3. Your glasses are __________.
4. John _________ finished the competition. He gave up at last.
5. I lost my bag. Can you help looking for it ______________ ?
6. Simon failed in the competition. He is __________ unhappy.
7. I saw her three hours ________ .
8. Mommy is cooking in the kitchen ________ .
9. We will have a barbecue _________________ .
10. Penny is ___________ talking on the phone.

挑戰站

請圈出句中的副詞，並判斷它的類別。

時間副詞（T）　地方副詞（P）　程度副詞（D）

1. Grandma took a walk in the park last week. ________
2. Uncle Peter put the book there. ________
3. Abbie did not do homework yesterday. ________
4. The puppy is very lovely. ________
5. Kerry and Grey are still talking in the meeting room. ________
6. Alice already left. ________
7. Benny had visited you a few days ago. ________
8. I just woke up and caught the bus. ________
9. Kenny and Mandy will get married next year. ________
10. Gordon is waiting for you there. ________

chapter 19

比較級的副詞

Adverbs: Comparative form of Adverbs

學校舉行班際歌唱比賽，皓皓的班和另一班要在決賽一較高下。台下聽眾說：「Class A is singing more softly than Class B.」，評判老師說：「Class B is more neatly than Class A.」。兩班實力相若，連評判都感到難以分出高下。

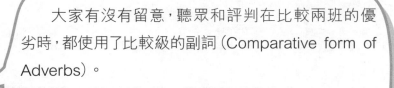

大家有沒有留意，聽眾和評判在比較兩班的優劣時，都使用了比較級的副詞（Comparative form of Adverbs）。

副詞跟形容詞一樣，可以將動作加以比較。副詞的比較也可以分為三個級別，即原級（Positive form）、比較級（Comparative form）和最高級（Superlative form）。

原級

原級即沒有比較，如「He runs fast.」（他跑得快。）副詞原級也可以用來指出同一個動作有兩種描述，沒分高低或級別，如「She speaks softly and clearly.」（她說得柔和而清楚。）

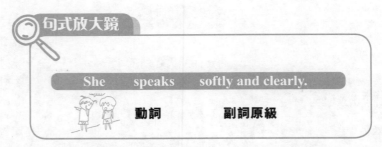

句式放大鏡

She	speaks	softly and clearly.
	動詞	副詞原級

上面的句子使用了副詞原級，即「softly and clearly」來描述她說話的動作。再看看其他例子：

He runs fast.
他跑得快。

Jack works hard.
積克辛勤地工作。

Stella writes well and neatly.
斯特拉寫得好和整齊。

比較級

比較級是比較同一動作但程度不同，常見的表達方式是「more＋副詞＋than」，如「Mary laughs more loudly than Kitty.」（瑪麗笑得比吉蒂更大聲。）

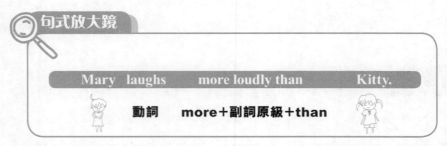

句式放大鏡

Mary	laughs	more loudly than	Kitty.
	動詞	more＋副詞原級＋than	

上面的句子使用了副詞比較級，即「more＋副詞原級＋than」來比較兩個小女孩的動作。再看看其他例子：

She sings better than Amy.
她唱得比艾美更好。

Miss Lee speaks more clearly than Miss Chan.
李老師說得比陳老師更清楚。

最高級

最高級是把三個或以上的動作作比較，從中分出「最......」的，常見的表達方式是「the most＋副詞」，如「He writes the most neatly in my class.」（在我班裡，他寫字寫得最整齊。）

句式放大鏡

He	writes	the most neatly	in my class.
	動詞	the most＋副詞原級	

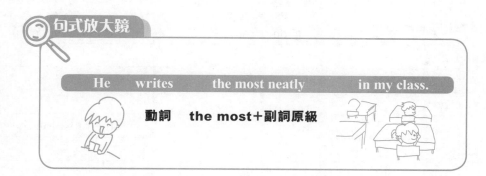

上面的句子使用了副詞最高級，即「the most＋副詞原級」，來指出在眾多同學之中，他寫字寫得最整齊。再看看其他例子：

Joyce makes the best cheese cake in the world.
在這世界上，喬依斯做的芝士蛋糕最好。

Jordon runs the fastest in Hong Kong.
在香港，佐敦跑得最快。

Shelly dances the most beautifully in my school.
在我的學校裡，雪梨跳舞跳得最漂亮。

大家可有留意到，當副詞要作不同級別的比較時，通常會將副詞原級作一定形式的變化，大家可參看下表：

副詞原級（Positive form）	副詞比較級（Comparative form）	副詞最高級（Superlative form）
單音節副詞：比較級在結尾加「-er」、最高級在結尾加「-est」		
fast（快速地）	faster（更快速地）	fastest（最快速地）
high（高高地）	higher（更高地）	highest（最高地）
兩個音節以上或結尾是「ly」的副詞：比較級是「more＋副詞原級＋than」、最高級是「the＋most＋副詞原級」		
usefully（有用地）	more usefully than（更有用地）	the most usefully（最有用地）
beautifully（漂亮地）	more beautifully than（更漂亮地）	the most beautifully（最漂亮地）
比較級和最高級不規則的副詞		
well（好好地）	better（更好地）	best（最好地）
badly（不好地）	worse（更不好地）	worst（最不好地）
early（早早地）	earlier（更早地）	earliest（最早地）

19 Adverbs: Comparative form of Adverbs

文法加油站

練習一

請寫出各級別的形容詞。

原級(Positive form)	比較級 (Comparative form)	最高級 (Superlative form)
1. carefully		
2.	better	
3. sweetly		
4.		the most loudly
5. softly		
6.	faster	
7. correctly		
8. high		
9. neatly		
10. nosily		
11.		the most quickly
12. poorly		
13. sadly		
14.	sooner	
15. silently		

練習二

請圈出句中的副詞，並判斷它的級別。

原級(P)　比較級(C)　最高級(S)

1. David runs faster than Peter. ______
2. Jack sings better than Ben. ______
3. Vanessa works hard. ______
4. Alison sings sweetly. ______
5. He writes well. ______
6. She seems sadly. ______
7. Johnny shouts the most loudly. ______
8. Joe gets the highest marks in my class. ______
9. Kitty did it poorly. ______
10. Mommy can make the best chocolate cake in the world. ______

挑戰站

參看例子，將提供的字詞放在句子的正確位置。

例子：We are late! We should leave. (immediately)
We are late! We should leave immediately.

1. Tommy does his homework at four o'clock. (always)

2. Jerry and Tammy go to the market. (seldom)

3. Please move the box. (carefully)

4. Amy is looking for her glasses. (everywhere)

5. Charles watches football match. (usually)

6. Please have the breakfast or we will miss the school bus. (quickly)

7. Mr. Smith will come to Hong Kong. (soon)

8. Mommy speaks to us. (softly)

9. Betty sings. (well and sweetly)

10. It rains. (suddenly)

chapter 20

前置詞：指示時間、位置、地點和動作

Preposition: showing positions, places, time and movements

小雲和朋友們在談論嘉莉，小雲說：「I saw Kelly at four o' clock.」（我在四時看到嘉莉。）小明說：「I saw Kelly in the library.」（我在圖書館見到嘉莉。）小賢說：「I saw Kelly going to the post office.」（我見到嘉莉去郵局。）小花說：「I saw Kelly walking around the park.」（我看到嘉莉在公園周圍散步。）

小雲和朋友們所說的話，都運用了前置詞（Preposition），如「at」（在……時間）、「in」（在……地方）、「to」（向……方向/地點）、「around」（在……周圍）。前置詞通常有特定的用法，大致可分為指示位置、指示地點、指示時間和指示動作四類。例如：

He made the model **on** Wednesday.
他在星期三完成了這個模型。

Judy stands **between** John and Amy.
茱迪站在約翰和艾美之間。

The supermarket is **opposite** to the post office.
圖書館在郵局對面。

Tom walked **along** the river yesterday.
昨天湯姆沿着小河散步。

句式放大鏡

He	made	the model	on	Wednesday.
	動詞		前置詞	表示時間的字詞

Judy	stands	between	John and Amy.
	動詞	前置詞	

The supermarket	is	opposite	to the post office.
	動詞	前置詞	

Tom	walked	along	the river	yesterday.
	動詞	前置詞		表示時間的字詞

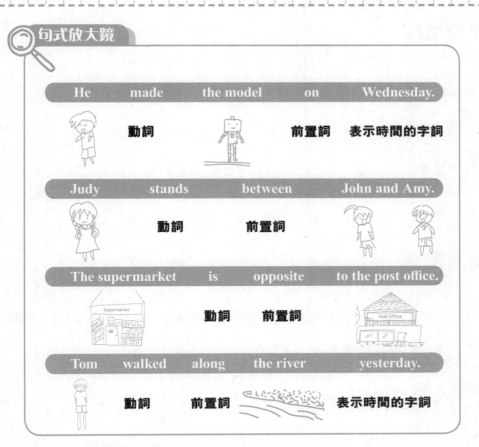

以上四個句子都使用了前置詞來指示時間、位置、地點和行動：

「He made the model on Wednesday.」句中的前置詞用來指示時間；

「The supermarket is opposite to the post office.」句中的前置詞用來指示地點；

「Judy stands between John and Amy.」句中的前置詞用來指示位置；

「Tom walked along the river yesterday.」句中的前置詞用來指示動作。

時間前置詞

指示時間的前置詞，除了「at」外，還有「in」（在……月份）、「on」（在星期……）、「for」（持續了……年）、「until」（直至……）等。例如：

I always wake up at seven o' clock.
我經常七時起床。

I was born in August.
我在八月出生。

Daddy does not work on Saturday and Sunday.
爸爸星期六和星期日不用工作。

We live here for three years.
我們在這兒已持續住了三年。

I can play football until four o' clock.
我可以踢足球直至四時。

位置前置詞

指示位置的前置詞，除了「between」外，還有「next to」（在……隔壁）、「near」（附近）、「at the top of」（在……頂部）等。例如：

My house is next to yours.
我的房子在你的隔壁。

The bus stop is near a school.
巴士站在學校附近。

The bird is at the top of the house.
那隻鳥在屋的頂部。

地點前置詞

指示地點的前置詞，除了「opposite」外，還有「in」（在……裡面）、「on」（在……上面）、「beside」（旁邊）、「in front of 」（在……前面）等。例如：

Joey and Jack are in the library.
祖兒和積克在圖書館。

The watch is on the table.
那隻手錶在桌上。

The cat is sitting beside Tammy.
那隻貓坐在譚美旁邊。

Sally is sitting in front of Sam.
莎莉坐在山姆前面。

動作前置詞

指示動作的前置詞，除了「along」外，還有「around」（周圍）、「across」（橫過）、「towards」（朝着）等。例如：

Grandma is walking around the park.
祖父在公園周圍散步。

Mandy is across the road.
蔓迪在過馬路。

The dog is walking towards the food.
那隻狗朝着食物走去。

常見的前置詞，如at、in、on很少有一種指示意義，它們既用於時間，也用於地點，大家使用時要留意這一點。

文法加油站

練習一

請圈出句中的前置詞。

1. His car is opposite to yours.
2. Christmas day is in December.
3. Mr. Chan walks across the road.
4. Mandy is walking toward Kenny.
5. Alex is walking around Tsim Sha Tsui East.
6. There is a cat at the top of the shelf.
7. I am standing between Peter and Gordon.
8. Henry lives here for ten years.
9. Mommy is in the kitchen.
10. The cat is sleeping on the sofa.

練習二

請根據右邊的中文譯句圈出正確的答案。

1. The bed is (at / near) the window.	這張床靠近窗。
2. The glass is (in / between) the pen and ruler.	水杯放在筆和尺的中間。
3. Raymond is walking (in / along) the swimming pool.	雷蒙正在泳池邊走。
4. Jessica is sitting (near / in front of) Ray.	杰西加坐在阿雷的前面。
5. The cat is walking (to / toward) the fish.	一隻貓正朝着那魚走去。
6. The orange is (at / next to) apple.	蘋果放在橙的旁邊。
7. The cross is (at the top of / in front of) the church.	教堂屋頂上有十字架。
8. The school is (near / opposite) to the church.	教堂對面是學校。
9. Amy has lunch (at / in) half past one.	艾美下午一點半時吃飯。
10. Raymond was born (at / in) May.	雷蒙在五月出生。

挑戰站

觀看地圖，寫出正確的答案。

1. A tree is ____________ Kerry's home.
2. The sport centre is ________________a small tree and a big tree.
3. The park is ________________ the bus stop and the supermarket.
4. The supermarket is _______________ the park.
5. The pet shop is ___________________the park.
6. The post office is ___________ the supermarket.
7. The pet shop is ___________________the post office.
8. Kerry's home is ______________ the sport centre.
9. The bus stop is ____________ the park.
10. A tree is ____________ the pet shop.

chapter 21

情態動詞的運用

Modals: can, could, may, might, shall, will, would, ought to

樂樂説：「I can draw.」（我會畫畫。）明明説：「You must clean the table.」（你必須清理桌面。）浩浩説：「Shall we go to swim tomorrow?」（我們明天去游泳嗎？）突然，小花大聲地説：「I will visit my grandma tomorrow. I can not go swimming with you.」（我明天將會探望祖母。我不可以和你們一起去游泳。）

樂樂和朋友們所説的話，都運用了情態動詞，如「must」（必須）、「can」（能、可以）、「shall」（將會）、「will」（將會）。甚麼是情態動詞（Modals）呢？**情態動詞通常用來表示説話人的情緒、態度或語氣**，雖然我們稱它為「動詞」，但是它不能單獨作動詞使用，所以有時會稱為「助動詞」。情態動詞必須後接動詞基本形，即「情態動詞＋動詞基本形」。例如：

Sam and Peter can come tomorrow.
山姆和彼得明天能來。

21 Modals: can, could, may, might , shall, will, would, ought to

句式放大鏡

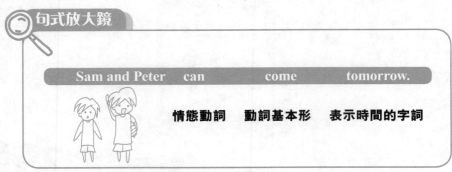

Sam and Peter	can	come	tomorrow.
	情態動詞	動詞基本形	表示時間的字詞

在「Sam and Peter can come tomorrow.」這個句子裡，情態動詞是「can」，後接動詞基本形「come」，大家留意主詞是不會影響情態動詞的。

情態動詞有哪些呢？「can（能、可以）、could（能、可以）、may（可能）、might（可能）、must（必須）、need（需要）、ought to（應該）、shall（應該、將會）、should（應該）、will（將會）、would（將會）」等都是情態動詞，它們的用途很廣泛，其中could、might、should、would等，用來表達更加客氣、委婉的語氣。

情態動詞的用法

(1) can和could表示能、可以、同意、准許，以及客觀條件許可的。

例如：Can you pass me the paper?
你能把紙遞給我嗎？

Could you help me?
請問你能幫助我嗎?

(2) may和might表示同意、許可或請求對方許可。might可表示過去式，或虛擬語氣，令言詞更加委婉、客氣，以及表示懷疑。

例如：May I use the computer?
我可以用這台電腦嗎？

The dog might be alive.
這條狗可能還活着。

(3) must的意思是必須、應該、一定，表示有必要做某事、命令、要求，以及對事物的推測。

例如：You must clean your room now.
你必須現在打掃你的房間。

It must be the dog John is looking for.
牠一定是約翰正在找的狗。

(4) ought to表示應該做某事。

例如：You ought to take grandpa to the hospital.
你應該帶祖父到醫院去。

(5) will和would表示將會做的事、決心和願望，也可以用於問句，表示向對方提出請求或詢問，而would的語氣比will更客氣。

例如：I will try my best.
我會盡力的。

Would you like some tea?
要喝點茶嗎？

(6) shall和should表示命令、警告、允諾、徵求、勸告、建議等。

例如：You should wake up now!
你現在應該起床了。

Shall we talk?
我們應該談談嗎?

肯定句、否定句和問句

情態動詞可用於肯定句、否定句和問句，例如：

(1) 肯定句形式

Joey and Tammy can sing.
祖兒和譚美能唱歌。

You must finish the homework by 4:00PM.
你必須在四時做完功課。

(2) 否定句形式

She can not come on time.
她不能準時到來。

David may not join the group.
大衛可能不加入那個小組。

(3) 問句形式

May I come in?
我可以進來嗎？

Shall we go now?
我們現在就去嗎？

can和could只能用於現在式和過去式，在將來式句子中只能用be able to（能、可以）來表示。must在過去式句子裡可以用had to來代替。另外，must和have to的主要區別在於must表示説話人的主觀思想，have to則表示客觀需要。

文法加油站

練習一

請參看例子，在情態動詞下畫底線，並把動詞圈出來。

例子： She can cook.

1. Dickson and Kenny may join us.
2. Would you pass me the pepper?
3. I must go to see Miss Lee now.
4. Could you give me your hand?
5. We ought to solve the problem as soon as possible.
6. Shall we go to hiking this Sunday?
7. Will you be teacher in the future?
8. She would like to have some sandwiches.
9. The weather will be getting worse.
10. John may arrive at six o' clock.

練習二

請圈出正確的答案。

1. Mr. Chan (could / would) like to have some coffee.
2. She (will / ought to) work in China at the end of this year.
3. I am late. I (should / will) go now.
4. (Shall / Must) we go to the beach?
5. He (must / will) finish the project by three o'clock.
6. Joey and Kelly (may / can) travel Japan this month.
7. Ken (must / may) wake up at six o'clock or he might miss the plane.
8. It (will / can) be sunny tomorrow.
9. You (should not / may not) watch the football match at mid night.
10. Amy and Simon (may / will) get married next month.

挑戰站

請參看例子，找出下列句子中的錯誤，並將正確的答案寫在右邊的橫線上。

例子：You should not played in the classroom. ______play______

1. Sam must finishing his homework by six o'clock. ____________
2. Penny will visited his grandparent this weekend. ____________
3. Miss Wong may gone to America next month. ____________
4. Shall we goes to hiking this Saturday? ____________
5. Would you passed me the book? ____________
6. I can playing piano. ____________
7. Chris should not watched TV at mid night. ____________
8. Sally and Joey may went to the library at 3:00PM. ____________
9. Kerry will not attended the meeting. ____________
10. Sam and Tammy will are nurse after graduation. ____________

chapter 22

疑問詞：放在問句的開頭

Question words: What, Where, Which, Who, How, Why

美兒是個愛發問的小女孩，常常問個不停：「What is that?」（這是甚麼？）「Where are the ants going?」（螞蟻去哪兒？）「When will the fish sleep?」（魚兒甚麼時候睡覺？）「Who is the tallest man in the world?」（誰是世界上最高的人？）

小朋友愛發問是一件好事，美兒所問的問題，都運用了疑問詞，如「Who」（誰）、「What」（甚麼）、「Where」（哪兒）、「When」（甚麼時候）。**疑問詞通常用來提問，或提出疑問**，以便取得更多資料。**它通常放在問句的開頭**，作起首詞。例如：

Who will come tomorrow?

誰明天會來？

句式放大鏡

Who	will	come	tomorrow?
疑問詞	助動詞	動詞基本形	表示時間的字詞

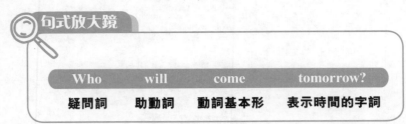

在這個句子裡，疑問詞是「Who」，放在問句的起首，大家要留意，以疑問詞起首作問句的句子，它的句末必須加上「?」。

疑問詞有哪些呢？

疑問詞有What（甚麼）、Where（哪兒）、Which（哪一個）、Who（誰）、Whom（誰）、Whose（誰的）、How（怎樣）、How many（多少）、How much（多少）、Why（為甚麼），等等。例如：

(1)Who, Whom, Whose：詢問人物

Who is your English teacher?
誰是你的英文老師？

Whom did you see in the party?
在那個派對裡，你見到誰？

Whose book is this?
這書是誰的？

(2)Which：詢問選擇

Which bag do you like, the red one or the white one?
你喜歡哪一個書包？紅色的，還是白色的？

Which one is beautiful, this one or that one?
哪一個漂亮，這個，還是那個？

(3)What：詢問事情、事件、事物等

What is typhoon?
甚麼是颱風？

What are you reading?
你在讀甚麼？

(4)When：詢問時間和日期

When is Christmas day?
甚麼時候是聖誕節？

When will you come?
你甚麼時候來？

(5)Where：詢問地點和位置

Where do you live?
你住在哪兒？

Where are you going?
你去哪兒？

(6)Why：詢問理由、原因

Why are you so sad?
為甚麼你不開心？

Why do you leave Hong Kong?
為甚麼你離開香港？

(7)How：詢問事物、行動的狀況，或進行的方式

How' s the show today?
今日的表演怎樣？

How are you?
你好嗎？

(8)How many和How much：詢問數量或數額

How many friends do you have?
你有多少個朋友？

How much is the book?
這書多少錢？

Who、Whom和Whose都是詢問人物，主要分別是Whom用作詢問提問人與聽話人以外的第三者，而Whose是詢問某物品的擁有者。

How many和How much的主要分別是，How many只用於詢問可以數算的事物，而How much則用於不可數算的事物。

文法加油站

練習一

下列疑問詞用來詢問甚麼內容？

How much ·	·人物
Why ·	·時間
Whom ·	·地點
Whose ·	·數量
Where ·	·事物的狀況
What ·	·數額
How many ·	·選擇
Who ·	·行動進行的方式
How ·	·日期
Which ·	·原因
When ·	·事情

練習二

請圈出正確的答案。

1. (Whom / What / Who) is Mr. Chan?
2. (What / Where / How) do you do?
3. (Whose / How many / Why) do you study in America?
4. (Whose / Which / Where) do you live?
5. (Whose / Which / Where) book is this?
6. (Who / Why /How much) did Joey get quarreled with Francis?
7. (How / What / Who) do you go to school?
8. (How / Whose / How many) pens do you need?
9. (How much / Who / What) is the watch?
10. (Whom / Whose / Who) did you meet in the party last night?

挑戰站

將正確的答案寫橫線上。

1. ____________ does grandpa wake up every morning?
He wakes up at six o'clock every morning.

2. ____________ does Penny live?
She lives in Lamma Island.

3. ____________ is your Chinese teacher?
Miss Wong is my Chinese teacher.

4. ____________ did you go hiking with last Saturday?
I went hiking with Judy last Saturday.

5. ____________ is the weather today?
It's sunny.

6. ____________ can Amy do?
She can play piano.

7. ____________ car it is?
It's Tom's.

8. ____________ is the bread?
It's five dollars.

9. ____________ does Kerry go?
He has to attend swimming class.

10. ____________ books do you have?
I have three books.

chapter 23

連接詞：連接詞語或句子

Connectives: and, or, but, so, because, so that, before, after

佩佩說：「I can draw and sing.」(我會畫畫和唱歌。) 峰峰說：「Do you like drawing or singing?」(你喜歡畫畫還是唱歌？) 茱迪說：「I am very busy in my homework but I am happy.」(我忙着做功課，但是我很開心。) 小花說：「I don' t like English because it is difficult.」(我不喜歡英文，因為它很難懂。)

上面小朋友所說的話，都運用了連接詞 (Connectives)，如「and」(和、及、並)、「or」(或者、否則)、「but」(但是)、「because」(因為)。甚麼是連接詞呢？**連接詞是用來連接字詞、片語或句子的詞語**，它在句中的位置會視乎字詞、片語或句子而定，有時會連接兩個名詞，有時連接兩個動詞，有時連接兩個句子。例如：

Tom and Judy are my friends.
湯姆和朱迪是我的朋友。
Miss Lee is angry because the students are lazy.
李老師生氣是因為學生們懶惰。

句式放大鏡

Tom and Judy are my friends.

連接詞

動詞

Miss Lee is angry because the students are lazy.

連接詞

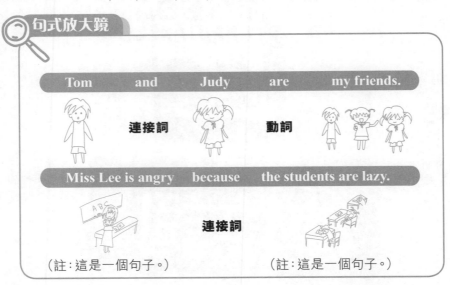

（註：這是一個句子。） （註：這是一個句子。）

在「Tom and Judy are my friends.」這個句子裡，連接詞是「and」（和、及），它把名詞「Tom」和「Judy」連接在一起，並成為句中的主詞。而「Miss Lee is angry because the students are lazy.」一句，連接詞是「because」（因為），它把原本是兩個獨立的完整句子，即「Miss Lee is angry.」和「The students are lazy.」連接在一起，成為一個表示因果關係的句子。

連接詞有哪些呢？「and」（和、及、並）、「or」（或者、否則）、「but」（但是）、「so」（所以）、「because」（因為）、「so that」（那麼）、「before」（...之前）、「after」（...之後），等等都是連接詞，它們的用法各有不同。

連接詞的用法

(1)「and」的意思是「和、及、並」，主要用來連接兩個事物，而這兩個事物通常在文法上是相似的，如名詞、形容詞等，大家可參看下圖：

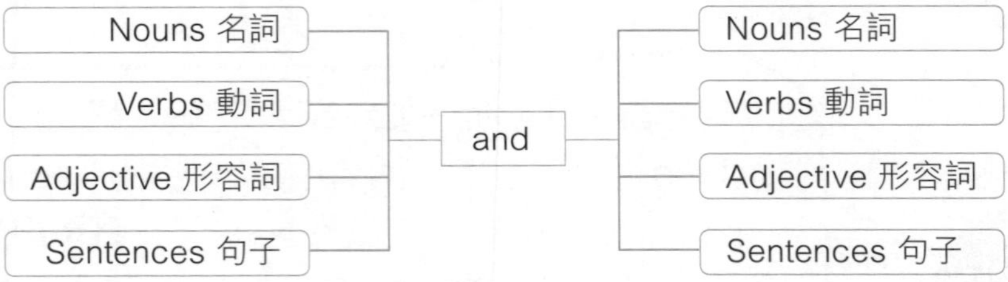

例如：

1. 名詞and名詞
Kelly and Alan are my sister and brother.
嘉莉和艾倫是我的姐姐和哥哥。

2. 動詞and動詞
The clock can ring and wake people up.
那個時鐘能響鬧及叫醒人們。

3. 形容詞and形容詞
Tommy is tall and smart.
湯姆又高又醒目。

4.句子and句子
Daddy likes coffee and mommy likes tea
爸爸喜歡咖啡，及媽媽喜歡茶。

(2) 「or」的意思是「或者、否則」，具有二選一和可能的意思。例如：

Is Nancy thin or fat?
南茜是瘦或肥？

Do you like coffee or tea?
你喜歡咖啡或茶？

You should work hard or you will fail in the examination.
你應該用功，否則你會考試不及格。

(3) 「but」的意思是「但是」，用來連接兩個相反的意思。例如：

Alice is slim but strong.
愛麗斯身段苗條但強壯。

It' s sunny but cool today.
今天天氣晴朗但清涼。

(4) 「so」的意思是「所以」，用來表示結果。例如：

I feel tired so I go to bed early.
我覺得疲倦，所以很早就睡覺。

You are lazy so you failed in the examination.
你懶惰，所以考試不合格。

(5) 「because」的意思是「因為」，用來帶出原因、理由。例如：

The children stay home because it' s raining.
孩子們留在家裡，因為外面下着雨。

Miss Lee gave me a small gift because I got 100 marks in English test.
李老師送給我一份小禮物，因為我英文測驗取得100分。

(6) 「so that」的意思是「那麼」，用來帶出目的。例如：

I join the party so that I can dance with Andy Lau.
我參加那個派對，那麼我就我可以跟劉德華跳舞。

Please give me some paper so that I can print out the document.
請給我一些紙，那麼我就可以把文件打印出來。

(7) 「before」和「after」的意思分別是「......之前」和「......之後」，用來表達動作或事情的先後次序。例如：

Joey washes her hand before she has lunch.
祖兒吃飯之前先洗手。

I watch TV after I finished my homework.
我做完功課之後看電視。

Please phone me before you come.
你來之前，請致電給我。

Sally eats ice cream after she had dinner.
莎莉吃完晚飯後吃冰淇淋。

大家使用「and」、「or」、「but」連接句子時，如果兩個句子的主詞和動詞是一樣的，可在第二句略去主詞和動詞，令句子顯得更簡潔。例如：

Tommy is tall. Tommy is handsome.
Tommy is tall and Tommy is handsome.
⇨Tommy is tall and handsome.

23 Connectives: and, or, but, so, because, so that, before, after

文法加油站

練習一

把句中的連接詞圈出來。

1. Kerry and Kelly will get married soon.
2. Do you like chocolate or strawberry cake?
3. I must go now or I will miss the train.
4. I can't go out because I have not finished my homework.
5. Please turn off the light before you leave the room.
6. I always go to bed after reading.
7. I do exercises every morning so that I can keep fit.
8. Grandpa is old but he is strong.
9. Greg went to the library and borrowed some books.
10. Who's your brother, Alex or Tom?

練習二

請圈出正確的答案。

1. Mr. Chan likes coffee (or / but / and) tea.
2. Where will she study, America (and / or / but) Canada?
3. Tammy should go now (but / or / and) she will be late.
4. It is a sunny day (because / so / so that) we go to the beach.
5. Johnny must finish the project (after / before / so that) his boss comes back from Jap
6. Kelly went to the supermarket (but / so / and) bought some food.
7. Ken have to wake up at six o'clock (or / so that / because) he can catch the flight to Beiji
8. The weather is sunny (and / but / or) cool today.
9. Tom should not watch football match (before / after / so) he finished the project.
10. Janice is fat (and / or / but) beautiful.

挑戰站

請參看例子，利用提供的字詞連接句子。

例子：You should not run in the classroom. You will be hurt. (or)
You should not run in the classroom or you will be hurt.

1. Sue must finish her homework. She can watch TV. (so that)

2. Peggy visited his grandparent. Peggy had dinner with them. (and)

3. Miss Fong is beautiful. Miss Fong is fat. (but)

4. Teddy and I went to hiking last Saturday. The weather was fine. (because)

5. Johnny is lazy. Johnny is unfriendly. (and)

6. The car is expensive. Uncle Ray will not buy it. (so)

7. Sammy works hard. Sammy can get high marks in the test. (so that)

8. You can play football. You can stay at home. (or)

9. Jerry did not attend the meeting this morning. Jerry was late. (because)

10. Lousia is happy. Amy is happy. (and)

全書練習答案

Chapter1 文法加油站

練習一

1. U 2. C 3. C 4. U 5. C 6. C 7. C 8. C 9. U 10. U 11. C 12. U 13. U 14. U 15. C

練習二

1. rabbits 2. oranges 3. wives 4. watches 5. heroes 6. books 7. pencils 8. bags
9. parties 10. thieves 11. flowers 12. wishes 13. dishes 14. babies 15. years

挑戰站

1. sisters 2. cups 3. uncles 4. beef 5. balls 6. tomatoes 7. universities
8. buses 9. trains 10. doctors 11. Italy 12. Hong Kong 13. Peter 14. dresses 15. China

Chapter2 文法加油站

練習一

1. It 2. He 3. They 4. You 5. her 6. me 7. They 8. We 9. They 10. It

練習二

1. Look at the dog. John is feeding it.

2. May has an apple. She will eat it after lunch.

3. Ken and Jerry are my friends. They like playing football.

4. The boy is making a car model. It will be finished later.

5. Annie is good at singing. Miss Wong chose her for the singing competition.

6. I need some pepper. Please pass it to me.

7. Johnny helps himself. He is a smart boy.

8. Peggy and Penny are good at painting. They will paint at the park this Sunday.

9. The pandas are cute. Let' s take some photos for them.

10. The chess class is fun. It was taught by Mr. Lam.

挑戰站

1. [They] It
2. [We] They
3. [He] She
4. [them] us
5. [He] They
6. [She] It
7. [She] They
8. [You] He
9. [He] It
10. [He] It

Chpater 3 文法加油站

練習一

1. itself 2. itself 3. herself 4. yourself 5. yourself 6. ourselves 7. themselves
8. myself 9. herself 10. itself

練習二

1. Look at the dog. It is scratching itself.
2. Vicky is drawing herself a picture.
3. Jerry and Chris are helping themselves on the problem.
4. Tom is making himself a craft.
5. Annie is keeping herself calm for a few minutes.
6. I am making myself an apple pie.
7. Johnny is a smart boy. He solves the problem himself.
8. Penny is dressing herself.
9. The panda fed its child itself.
10. Teddy encourages himself for the competition.

挑戰站

1. [itselves] itself
2. [themselves] himself
3. [yourself] herself
4. [themselves] ourselves
5. [herself] himself
6. [himself] herself
7. [yourselves] himself
8. [ourselves] yourself / yourselves
9. [himself] herself
10. [himself] themselves

Chapter 4 文法加油站

練習一

1. This/That 2. These/Those 3. This/That 4. These/Those 5. This/That 6. These/Those
7. This/That 8. These/Those 9. These/Those 10. This/That

練習二

1. These 2. That 3. This 4. That 5. That 6. That 7. Those 8. That 9. Those 10. This

挑戰站

1. He 2. me 3. She 4. himself 5. It 6. They 7. herself 8. us 9. This/That 10. These/Those

Chapter 5 文法加油站

練習一

1. Mommy is cleaning Kitty's room.
2. This is my father's car.
3. Tracy borrowed Miss Lee's book.
4. The boys' English teacher is Mr. Smith.
5. Karen's daddy brought her a computer game.
6. Kathy's mommy goes to the supermarket.
7. This is Teddy's dog.
8. I am using Kerry's mobile.
9. Peter's sister is Sue.
10. That is Amy's watch.

練習二

1. These are the holes of the bottle.
2. These are the legs of the chair.
3. These are the characters of the game.
4. This is the cover of the magazine.
5. These are the windows of the flat.
6. These are the doors of the house.
7. These are the ears of the dog.
8. These are the wheels of the car.
9. These are the flowers of the garden.
10. This is the end of the film.

挑戰站

1. [Cherry room] Cherry's room
2. [on] of
3. [dog tail] dog's tail
4. [the bed's legs] the legs of the bed
5. [The old man grandchild] The old man's grandchild
6. [Jessica picture] Jessica's picture
7. [Fred toy cars] Fred's toy cars
8. [the book's cover] the cover of the book
9. [the car's wheels] the wheels of the car
10. [The children story books] The children's story books

Chapter 6 文法加油站

練習一

1. This is his car model.
2. This is her house.
3. This is its dog house.
4. This is their car.
5. These are our computers.
6. These are your bags.
7. These are my books.
8. This is their boat.
9. These are their toys.
10. These are your pictures.

練習二

1. their 2. their 3. her 4. our 5. her 6. his 7. its 8. his 9. my 10. Her

挑戰站

1. [their] our
2. [his] her
3. [His] Its
4. [your] my
5. [our] her
6. [its] their
7. [his] her
8. [our] my
9. [his] their
10. [their] her

Chapter 7 文法加油站

練習一

1. The car model is his.
2. The house is hers.
3. The dog house is its.
4. The car is theirs.
5. The computers are ours.
6. The bags are yours.
7. The books are mine.
8. The boat is theirs.
9. The toys are theirs.
10. The pictures are yours.

練習二

1. This is my dog. It is mine.
2. This is Ricky's bag. This is his.
3. This is Jerry and Ann's house. This is theirs.
4. This is Tom's car model. This is his.
5. This is the dog's house. This is its.
6. This is my cup. This is mine.
7. These are your books. These are yours.
8. This is Penny's dress. This is hers.
9. This is Mr. Leung's car. That is his.
10. This is our house. This is ours.

挑戰站

1. His 2. hers 3. 's 4. my 5. of 6. theirs 7. 's 8. our 9. Its 10. its

Chapter 8 文法加油站

練習一

1. an 2. a 3. a 4. a 5. an 6. a 7. a 8. a 9. an 10. a

練習二

1. a 2. an 3. a 4. a 5. an 6. a 7. an 8. a 9. an 10. an

挑戰站

1. There is <an> apple on the table.
2. <A> cup is on the book shelf.
3. I have <an> orange.
4. There is <a> university in Shatin.
5. You have <an> hour to do homework.
6. There is <an> elephant in the zoo.
7. <A> boy is standing under the tree.
8. There is <a> girl in the classroom.
9. <A> book is under the chair.
10. There is <an> umbrella in the basket.

Chapter 9 文法加油站

練習一

1. The 2. X. 3. the 4. The 5. The 6. The 7. the 8. the 9. the 10. the

挑戰站

1. a 2. an 3. an 4. the 5. X 6. the 7. The 8. the 9. a 10. the 11. The 12. The
13. the 14.The 15. a 16. the 17. The 18.a 19. The 20. the

Chapter 10 文法加油站

練習一

1. is 2. are 3. borrowed 4. did 5. have 6. lives 7. bought 8. sit 9. played 10. is

練習二

1. do 2. is 3. am 4. have 5. are 6. does 7. do 8. have 9. are 10. has

挑戰站

1. does 2. do 3. has 4. is 5. are 6. are 7. have 8. am 9. is 10. has

Chapter 11 文法加油站

練習一

Verbs	Yesterday	Today	Tomorrow
1. be	was, were	am, is, are	will be
2. have	had	has, have	will have
3. sing	sang	sing	will sing
4. run	ran	run	will run
5. go	went	go	will go
6. play	played	play	will play
7. talk	talked	talk	will talk
8. join	joined	join	will join
9. drink	drank	drink	will drink
10. write	wrote	write	will write

練習二

1. P 2. F 3. PS 4. P 5. PS 6. F 7. P 8. PS 9. P 10. P

挑戰站

1. play 2. will work 3. will move 4. went 5. were 6. was 7. had 8. does 9. am 10. likes

Chapter 12 文法加油站

練習一

1. [were] I 2. [went] I 3. [did] I 4. [played] R 5. [had] I
6. [visited] R 7. [was] I 8. [danced] R 9. [was] I 10. [flew] I

練習二

1. visited 2. danced 3. was 4. had 5. did 6. saw 7. told 8. came 9. talked 10. sang

挑戰站

1. sat 2. ran 3. read 4. listened 5. spoke 6. swam 7. thought 8. ate 9. gave
10. felt 11. built 12. showed 13. rode 14. put 15. wore 16. cut 17. saw 18. went

Chapter 13 文法加油站

練習一

. She dislikes swimming.
2. Kelly and Amy begin crying.
. Please stop talking.
4. He likes smoking.
. I hate doing homework.
6. Alice and Tim enjoy singing.
. He suggests going to China.
8. Please keep doing exercise.
. Michael likes cooking.
10. Judy dislikes making models.

練習二

. staying 2. having 3. swimming 4. buying 5. breaking 6. going 7. eating
. thinking 9. making 10. playing

挑戰站

1. [keep] keeping　2. [run] running　3. [do] doing　4. [read] reading
5. [drink] drinking　6. [give] giving　7. [work] working　8. [eat] eating
9. [cry] crying

Chapter 14 文法加油站

練習一

1. I need to drink something.
2. Hong Kong people love to eat Japanese food.
3. Johnny agrees to go hiking with us.
4. Kerry needs to do homework at four o' clock.
5. Please let me know what happened.
6. The fat man should begin to keep fit now.
7. I try to see you this weekend.
8. Kitty hates to do homework.
9. Mr. Wong wants to buy a new computer.
10. Mandy helps her child to wash hair.

練習二

1. see 2. to arrive 3. to swim 4. to buy 5. to go 6. to go 7. know 8. tell 9. to eat 10. wash

挑戰站

1. show　2. playing　3. making　4. drawing　5. rush
6. Swimming　7. to meet　8. breaking　9. visiting　10. to study

Chapter 15 文法加油站

練習一

1. childish　2. careful /careless　3. famous　4. foolish　5. beautiful
6. useful / useless　7. bookish　8. enjoyable　9. valuable　10. dependent
11. musical　12. different　13. national　14. creative　15. active

練習二

1. [three] 2. [his] 3. [expensive] 4. [This] 5. [last] 6. [big] 7. [beautiful] 8. [many]
9. [Those] 10. [His]

挑戰站

1. [one] AQy　2. [my] PA　3. [interesting] AQ　4. [Those] DA
5. [first] AQy　6. [beautiful] AQ　7. [smart] AQ　8. [some] AQy
9. [These] DA　10. [Our] PA

Chapter 16 文法加油站

練習一

原級（Positive form）	比較級（Comparative form）	最高級（Superlative form）
1. careful	more careful	the most careful
2. hardworking	more hardworking	the most hardworking
3. interesting	more interesting	the most interesting
4. pretty	prettier	prettiest
5. hot	hotter	hottiest
6. cold	colder	coldest
7. cheap	cheaper	cheapest
8. expensive	more expensive	the most expensive
9. fat	fatter	fattest
10. sad	sadder	saddest
11. good	better	the best
12. bad	worse	worst
13. many	more	most
14. much	more	most
15. little	less	least

練習二

1. [smarter] C
2. [beautiful] P
3. [funny] P
4. [the most beautiful] S
5. [laziest] S
6. [small] P
7. [fat] P
8. [tallest] S
9. [more hardworking] C
10. [worst] S

挑戰站

1. best 2. more 3. big 4. cute 5. oldest 6. shorter 7. more helpful 8. laziest
9. more expensive 10. worse

Chapter 17 文法加油站

練習一

1. [carelessly] 2. [always] 3. [busily] 4. [easily] 5. [carefully] 6. [softly] 7. [seldom]
8. [sometimes] 9. [weekly] 10. [never]

練習二

1. loudly 2. never 3. carelessly 4. clearly 5. quietly 6. always 7. carefully 8. softly
9. suddenly 10. worse

挑戰站

1. [slowly] (M)
2. [seldom] (F)
3. [carelessly] (M)
4. [easily] (M)
5. [softly] (M)
6. [quietly] (M)
7. [sometimes] (F) / [late] (M)
8. [sometimes](F)
9. [suddenly] (M)
10. [monthly] (F)

Chapter 18 文法加油站

練習一

1. [very] 2. [everywhere] 3. [here] 4. [ago] 5. [quite] 6. [very] 7. [just] 8. [today]
9. [everywhere] 10. [next month]

練習二

1. there /here 2. too 3. here/there 4. almost 5. everywhere 6. very 7. ago 8. now
9. tomorrow 10. still

挑戰站

1. [last week] (T)
2. [there] (P)
3. [yesterday] (T)
4. [very] (D)
5. [still] (T)
6. [already] (T)
7. [ago] (T)
8. [just] (D)
9. [next year] (T)
10. [there] (P)

Chapter 19 文法加油站

練習一

原級 (Positive form)	比較級 (Comparative form)	最高級 (Superlative form)
1. carefully	more carefully	the most carefully
2. well	better	the best
3. sweetly	more sweetly	the most sweetly
4. loudly	more loudly	the most loudly
5. softly	more softly	the most softly
6. fast	faster	fastest
7. correctly	more correctly	the most correctly
8. high	higher	highest
9. neatly	more neatly	the most neatly
10. nosily	more nosily	the most nosily
11. quickly	more quickly	the most quickly
12. poorly	more poorly	the most poorly
13. sadly	more sadly	the most sadly
14. soon	sooner	soonest
15. silently	more silently	the most silently

練習二

1. [faster] C
2. [better] C
3. [hard] P
4. [sweetly] P
5. [well] P
6. [sadly] P
7. [the most loudly] S
8. [highest] S
9. [poorly] P
10. [best] S

挑戰站

1. Tommy always does his homework at four o' clock.
2. Jerry and Tammy seldom go to the market.
3. Please move the box carefully.
4. Amy is looking for her glasses everywhere.
5. Charles usually watches football match.
6. Please have the breakfast quickly or we will miss the school bus.
7. Mr. Smith will come to Hong Kong soon.
8. Mommy speaks to us softly.
9. Betty sings well and sweetly.
10. It suddenly rains.

Chapter 20 文法加油站

練習一

1. [opposite] 2. [in] 3. [across] 4. [toward] 5. [around] 6. [at the top of] 7. [between] 8. [for] 9. [in] 10. [on]

練習二

1. near 2. between 3. along 4. in front of 5. toward 6. next to 7. at the top of 8. opposite 9. at 10. in

挑戰站

1. near 2. between 3. between 4. near 5. opposite to 6. opposite to 7. near 8. opposite to 9. next to 10. near

Chapter 21 文法加油站

練習一

1. Dickson and Kenney may join us.
2. Would you pass me the pepper?
3. I must go to see Miss Lee now.
4. Could you give me your hand?
5. We ought to solve the problem as soon as possible.
6. Shall we go to hiking this Sunday?
7. Will you be teacher in the future?
8. She would like to have some sandwiches.
9. The weather will be getting worse.
10. John may arrive at six o' clock.

練習二

1. would 2. will 3. should 4. Shall 5. must 6. may 7. must 8. will 9. should not 10. will

挑戰站

1. [finishing] finish
2. [visited] visit
3. [gone] go
4. [goes] go
5. [passed] pass
6. [playing] play
7. [watched] watch
8. [went] go
9. [attended] attend
10. [are] be

Chapter 22 文法加油站

練習一

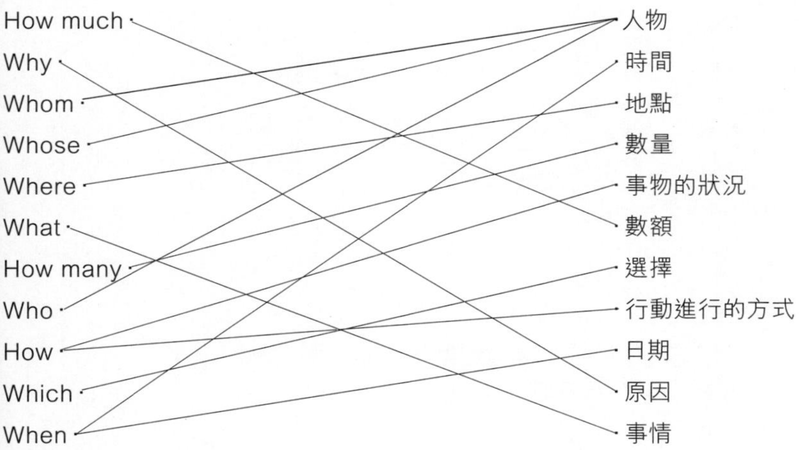

練習二

1. Who 2. What/How 3. Why 4. Where 5. Whose 6. Why 7. How 8. How many 9. How much 10. Whom

挑戰站

1. When 2. Where 3. Who 4. Whom 5. How 6. What 7. Whose 8. How much 9. Why 10. How many

Chapter 23 文法加油站

練習一

1. [and] 2. [or] 3. [or] 4. [because] 5. [before] 6. [after] 7. [so that] 8. [but] 9. [and] 10. [or]

練習二

1. and 2. or 3. or 4. so 5. before 6. and 7. so that 8. but 9. before 10. but

挑戰站

1. Sue must finish her homework so that she can watch TV.
2. Peggy visited his grandparent and had dinner with them.
3. Miss Fong is beautiful but fat.
4. Teddy and I went to hiking last Saturday because the weather was fine.
5. Johnny is lazy and unfriendly.
6. The car is expensive so Uncle Ray will not buy it.
7. Sammy works hard so that she can get high marks in the test.
8. You can play football or stay at home.
9. Jerry did not attend the meeting this morning because he was late.
10. Lousia and Amy are happy.

《小學生學 Grammar——圖解教程和練習 (詞語文法)》

編著：李雪熒
責任編輯：蘇飛、李卓蔚
封面及版面設計：麥碧心
插圖：王美琪
協力：李美儀

出版：跨版生活圖書出版
地址：荃灣沙咀道 11-19 號達貿中心 211 室
電話：3153 5574　　　　傳真：3162 7223
專頁：http://www.facebook.com/crossborderbook
網站：http://www.crossborderbook.net
電郵：crossborderbook@yahoo.com.hk

發行：泛華發行代理有限公司
地址：香港新界將軍澳工業邨駿昌街 7 號星島新聞集團大廈
電話：2798 2220　　　　傳真：2796 5471
網頁：http://www.gccd.com.hk
電郵：gccd@singtaonewscorp.com

台灣總經銷：永盈出版行銷有限公司
地址：231 新北市新店區中正路 499 號 4 樓
電話：(02)2218 0701　　　　傳真：(02)2218 0704

印刷：鴻基印刷有限公司

出版日期：2021 年 3 月第三版
定價：HK$88 NT$350
ISBN：978-988-78897-1-7

出版社法律顧問：勞潔儀律師行